CHAOS IN CARPATHIA

CHAOS IN CARPATHIA!
GOTHIC HORROR SKIRMISH BATTLES

By Scott R. Pyle

Playtesting and Development: Louis Reash, Aaron Tobul, Lee Howard, Brian Botzan, Scott Crane, Bill Demjan, Jerry Frazee, Jim Hoffman, Sky Hernstrom, Enrico Nardini, Agis Neugebauer, Tom Weiss, and Thomas Whitten

Character Designs: Bob Naismith and Scott Pyle

Figure Designs: Bob Naismith

General Inspiration: Russ Dunaway

Layout and Design: Daniel Yauger

Short Fiction: Sky Hernstrom and Scott Pyle

Special Thanks: JoAnn Rizzo

Interior Illustrations by Rich Yanizeski, Dan Horsechief, and from the public domain

Cover Painting by Christopher Moeller

Photos courtesy of istockphoto.com

Publisher: Four-Color Figures, 2007

For More Information Contact:

Four-Color Figures
Box 20, Rt. 981
Calumet, PA 15621
1-724-423-3580
http://www.oldgloryminiatures.com
fourcolorfigs@yahoo.com

Table of Contents

Carpathian Mountains, 1888

Amidst the cold and forbidding mountains of Eastern Europe a battle that could decide the fate of humanity wages between men and monsters.

November 3, 1888
The Carpathian Mountains

The cave passage was dank, cold, and confining, but Sir Godfrey Hampton was glad to be out of the driving storm that had plagued his company since their departure from Danova just two days ago. The flickering glow of the lantern clasped in the sodden Englishmen's right hand cast wan light on his companions. They followed behind him down the narrow passage, trying for all they could to move silently, but few could even keep their teeth from chattering. Even out of the wind and the wet the cave was cold. In the light Nicolao Hunyadi could see his breath. He stayed close to Hampton, one gloved hand on his revolver, the other clasping a wooden stake that carried the blessings of four local clerics and Danova's town drunk, just for good measure.

Hunyadi's wide-brimmed hat dripped cold water onto the stubble of his unshaven chin, a steady drip that bespoke of how long they had traveled and how desperate they were.

Had they arrived first? Carolina Pickard asked herself again, her unvoiced question echoing the thoughts of her comrades. She too was soaked through to her knickers, and she had to resist the urge to again unfold the drenched map and consult it one last time. Was this the right cave? She thought to herself again, but instead of pulling the map she drew a pistol instead and quietly checked to make sure it was dry enough to fire.

Behind her Radu Barbu cursed quietly to himself. He could have stayed behind in Danova, but his debt to Hampton had compelled him to come along. In truth guilt was his greatest compulsion, for it had been his hidden delving that awakened the threat of the Nameless Ones. His vaunted scholarship and research had been watched by evil eyes. The foes of man learned of the hidden Sepulcher of the Nameless Gods after Barbu had pieced its location together from numerous ancient sources. They had seduced him using one of their young servants, and he had given them the information willingly. And then they had tried to kill him. Barbu brought his chubby, water-wrinkled hand up to the twin puncture marks on his thick neck. The wounds had finally begun to scab over after weeping blood for nearly a week. There was much to atone for.

"The passage widens ahead," Hampton called back to his companions in a harsh whisper. "Be on your guard!" No sooner did the warning come than the space ahead of the Englishman filled with a large dark shape set off by a pair gleaming red eyes.

"So glad you could come, Hampton," a familiar voice mocked from the darkness. It was Mladic, the Blood Servant's voice. And as he spoke Hampton held his lamp a little higher, and beyond Mladic's gaunt form the passage room was filled with other shambling figures. They had lost the race, but would they now lose the coming battle?

~1~

The Basics

INTRODUCTION

CHAOS IN CARPATHIA (CIC) IS A FAST-PACED, skirmish-level miniatures battle game designed to simulate clashes between men and monsters in the Victorian era. Following in the tradition of classic tales like Dracula, the Werewolf, and Frankenstein, CIC allows players to fight epic battles pitting heroes against villains.

Playing a game of CIC requires the following: a copy of these rules, painted miniatures, around 10 six-sided dice, copies of the warband roster sheet from the back of this book, pencils, and a roughly 4' x 4' playing area. Chaos in Carpathia can be played with 2 or more players.

Battles in Chaos in Carpathia generally involve about five to ten models per side. There are two basic types of models in the game: characters and henchmen. Characters are the heroes and villains that star in the action-packed tales of the old Victorian penny-dreadfuls. Henchmen are their underlings, goons, nameless minions, or cannon fodder.

The characters and rules of Chaos in Carpathia allow players to tell a collective story on the tabletop, with models taking on the roles of heroes and villains who will develop unique personalities, overcome obstacles, and sometimes suffer grievous injuries. These developments occur over a number of game sessions, and are called campaign games. Chapter VII of this booklet contains rules for running these interlocked scenarios.

The Basics

ELDER RUMBLINGS

During the reign of Ladislaus I., King of Hungary (1078-95), who conquered the Kumans, Transylvania was united with Hungary, and began for the first time to enjoy the blessings of peace and order. It had long been whispered by some that Ladislaus had made a bargain with some sinister power to make this peace last. Further evidence of this deadly pact emerged more than a century later when Andreas I. (1204-35) made it known to his associates in the Teutonic Order that they must leave the land in 1225.

Andreas kept at his side a mysterious advisor whose visage was always shrouded in the shadows of a great cowl. Nicolaus von Draken was his name. He whispered dark poison in Andreas' ear about the order of the Teutons, and their relationship with Honorius III. And so they were expelled. But dark pacts are fickle things, and decades of peace can melt away like a snowfall in late spring. Transylvania's darkest days were still ahead of her.

GAME MECHANICS

THE MOST IMPORTANT RULE

Chaos in Carpathia is your game. If you don't like the way something works, discuss it with your gaming group and make a change that is acceptable to everyone.

THE GOAL ROLL

The heart of CIC is the Goal Roll. Most actions in the game require a goal roll, and during every goal roll a model has a certain number, or pool of dice which its player must roll. The player rolls the dice and looks for dice rolling 4 or greater (i.e., 4, 5, or 6); this will determine the number of goals collected in that throw. Dice rolling less than 4 are ignored.

Example: *Sir Godfrey Hampton wishes to strike a foe in Close Combat. He rolls 5 dice and gets a 2, 3, 4, 4, and 5, for a total of 3 Goals.*

Models in CIC possess four basic attributes rated by a number of dice. The four attributes are Strength, Agility, Mind, and Resolve. For example, a model with Agility 3 would roll three dice to strike a target in close combat or at range. As stated above, any die rolling 4+ counts toward the total goals scored, and lower die rolls are ignored.

THE POWER OF 6

Rolling a 6 in CIC is special. Whenever a model rolls a 6 on a throw it counts as two goals.

Example: *Mladic the Blood Servant's player rolls his five Strength dice and gets 1, 3, 4, 4, and 6 for a total of four goals.*

RE-ROLLS

Some special traits and equipment allow players to re-roll failed dice for their models. For an easy reminder, the number of re-rolls allowed on a throw can be noted in brackets next to the relevant attribute or dice pool. For example, a player running a vampire with 5 dice in Strength and immunity to firearms would get 3 re-rolls on damage resistance and note them thusly: DR 5D[3]. Re-rolls may be used on each throw of the relevant dice pool.

UNOPPOSED GOAL ROLLS

In an unopposed goal roll, the player rolls a number of dice equal to her model's relevant attribute, and counts up the number of goals. At least one goal is needed to succeed at the minimum level.

Example: *Heroine Carolina Pickard is trying to leap a 2" chasm. She possesses Strength 3, and so her player rolls 3 dice, getting 1, 2, and 5 for one goal, just enough to make it to the other side.*

TARGET NUMBERS

Certain values in CIC are fixed, and require no dice rolling. These values normally represent target numbers that opposing models must resist with an Unopposed Goal Roll. This most often reflects the action of combat, where a model struck by an attack must resist the attack's target number or suffer damage. See the combat section below for more details. In combat situations, target numbers

are denoted as Damage Numbers, or "DN#". In other circumstances, target numbers are denoted as "TN#".

OPPOSED GOAL ROLLS

Some of the most important goal rolls in CIC are Opposed Goal Rolls. When one model attacks another, the attacker's relevant attribute is pitted against the defender's relevant attribute in an opposed contest. The model that gains more goals (dice rolling 4+) wins the contest, and in the case of combat, might successfully strike or dodge. In some cases, a model's net goals are added to the effects of its action. For example, in combat, a model that successfully strikes a foe and beats his total by 3+ goals adds +1 to the attack's DN. In all opposed goal rolls, ties go to the defender.

Example: *Hampton and the Blood Servant Mladic battle amidst the frozen fir trees of a Carpathian pass. Hampton attacks with Agility 3, and so his player rolls 3 dice getting 1, 4, and 6 for three goals. Mladic's player rolls his Agility 3 and gets a 2, 3, and 5 for only one goal. Hampton wins three goals to one, a solid hit!*

ROUNDING

Whenever a rule or situation calls for a model to halve a trait, players round numbers up normally. For example, a value of 3 halved is 1.5, which would be rounded up to 2.

THE ANATOMY OF A WARRIOR

THE FOUR ATTRIBUTES

Chaos in Carpathia characters are made up of four primary attributes rated in numbers of dice. They are as follows:

Strength: Physical power and damage resistance capacity.

Agility: Nimbleness, skill in close combat and accuracy at range.

Mind: Perception, intelligence, and mental acuity.

Resolve: Willpower, courage, resistance to pain and magical attacks.

The normal human maximum for individual attributes is 4. Models possessing certain special traits may exceed this maximum.

OTHER VALUES

Beyond the four attributes, several other values play an important role in defining a CIC character. Unlike attributes, some of these values are not rated in terms of numbers of dice.

Move: A model's Move value represents the number of inches it may move during its turn.

Special Traits: Special Traits define the extra skills and amazing abilities models possess. Many traits are available to models, and all are listed in Chapter V.

DR: Damage Resistance--number of dice equal to 1 + Strength attribute.

Fate: Some Character models possess a spirit and a will to live that grants them an amazing tenacity and resistance. A model's Fate is equal to its starting Resolve, and represents a number of free dice a model may add to important rolls during the course of a game. A model must announce it is using Fate before

---

OTHER USES OF FATE

A model's Fate can be the most critical tool in its battle for survival on the tabletop. In addition to adding dice in key situations, a model may also spend its Fate to perform an additional Attack or Special action during its turn. Gaining an additional Attack or Special action costs 2 Fate dice.

A model may also use Fate to extend its Move for the turn. Each die of fate adds 2" of Move value for that turn. This can be used in addition to a charge maneuver, and need not be declared at the beginning of the model's turn. Charge that fall short and are subsequently increased by fate still count as charges.

The Basics

any dice are rolled, and once they have been spent, they are gone for the remainder of the game. A model's Fate dice refresh at the beginning of each new game.

Vitality: Vitality measures a model's health, or how many hits the model can take before it goes down. Most character models start the game with 3 Vitality. Certain character models may possess Special Traits that alter this base number. Henchmen groups handle damage and Vitality loss differently and are covered in Chapter III.

~2~

Combat and Movement

THE COMBAT ROUND

L IKE MOST MINIATURES GAMES, Chaos in Carpathia features a specific sequence of events that helps to organize the chaos of heroic action. This sequence is known as the Combat Round, or Round for short. Unlike some other games, a CIC round is broken down into only two phases:

1.) Initiative
2.) Actions

These two phases transform the chaos of cinematic combat into a playable and orderly game turn.

ROUNDS AND TURNS

In CIC, a Round consists of a number of Turns equal to the number of character models and henchmen groups involved in the battle. Each model gets a Turn to activate.

INITIATIVE

T he Initiative phase in CIC determines the order in which models will take their turns. When the last model to act in a round has completed its last action, a new round begins with the Initiative phase.

CIC presents two distinct methods for determining Initiative. Before a game players should decide which method to use and stick to it for the remainder of the game. Each method

Combat and Movement

has its merits, and players should give both a try to determine the one they like better.

INITIATIVE METHOD I- CARD BASED

When determining Initiative, a standard deck of 54 playing cards (counting Jokers) should be employed, and every character model and henchmen group receives a minimum of one card to determine initiative.

Each round players should take turns dealing from the deck to each character model or henchmen group. When the cards from the deck are exhausted, players should shuffle the discarded cards from previous rounds and begin dealing anew. Cards are dealt face-up and turn order is determined by the value of each card in the following manner:

> Joker (first)
> Ace
> King
> Queen
> Jack
> 10 - 2

Comparing the cards' suits breaks any ties:

> Clubs (1st)
> Diamonds (2nd)
> Hearts (3rd)
> Spades (4th)

Certain characters or henchmen groups might possess special traits that give them more cards, but a model or models only ever counts one card (the highest) when determining initiative, all others are ignored. After the last model has acted each round, the player who didn't deal last round deals a fresh set of cards to each model still participating in the battle. KO'ed models always act last when using this system, no matter what card they are dealt.

INITIATIVE METHOD II- DICE BASED

Before the battle begins, each player designates one of his models as the Leader of his team. At the beginning of each Round, each player makes an Initiative goal roll for his leader.

Leaders possess Initiative dice equal to their Mind attribute. The leader who scores the higher number of goals wins the initiative for that round and may decide whether he wishes to activate one of his models first that round, or whether he wishes to defer to his opponent.

Ties are broken by comparing Mind attribute totals. If Mind totals are tied, then players should each roll a single D6 until one of them scores a higher roll.

When one model activates it takes its turn, then a model from the opposing force activates and takes its turn, and so on until all models have taken their turn for that round.

MULTIPLE LEADERS

When a team's leader is KO'ed or taken out of action, its player must choose another model from the team as the new leader.

ACTIONS

There are four types of actions in CIC: Move, Free, Combat, and Special. Models may perform one Move action, and either one special or one combat action per turn. Models may perform a number of Free actions up to their Mind attribute rating.

MOVE ACTIONS

Every model in CIC gets a Move Action during its turn. Models can cover up to a number of inches equal to their Move value. A model may split this up over the course of its turn, interspersing this movement with the performance of other actions.

> The card-based initiative creates a much more dynamic and wild version of the game, and may alter the way a given warband plays. The unpredictable nature of card draws and the sheer table space the cards tend to take up makes for a messier game, but one that is no less fun than the dice-based initiative.

Combat and Movement

Measuring & Base Contact

Chaos in Carpathia movements are all measured in inches, and measurements are taken from the edge of the model's base to the edge of an opposing model's base (in the case of measuring distances for charges and ranged combat). Base Contact occurs when one model's base touches another model's base. This is normally the only way enemy models may fight close combat.

Pre-Measuring

The fast action of Chaos in Carpathia does not allow for time for pre-measuring distances. When making ranged attacks or determining distance for charges, it is up to a player's judgment whether or not he has the range or movement to meet his goal. The intent to move or attack is first declared, and then range is measured. If the goal is outside the move or range, the model stops short or the shot goes awry.

Facing

Facing is never an issue in Chaos in Carpathia; it is always assumed that a model can see 360 degrees around itself. A model may expend a free action to change its facing.

Charging

A Charge is a type of Move action. Models who charge add 5" to their Move value for movement for that turn. A model charges to either cover extra ground, or meet a foe in close combat. Charging models run all out, and may do nothing else that turn. However, charging models that make it into base contact with another model can make one attack on the model at +2 dice.

A model charging a foe must move at least the last 3" in a straight line in order to receive the +2 dice bonus. A model that charges and attacks a foe at the end of its charge is essentially combining its Move and Combat actions for its turn, and can do no other combat or special actions that round. Certain free actions like searching for hidden models may still be attempted prior to charging. Models that charge to cover extra ground can do nothing else but move and perform free actions during their turn.

Charging is the most common method of entering Close Combat. A model must declare that it is attempting to charge an enemy model before measuring the distance between them. A model may charge an enemy that it cannot see because of terrain or other factors, but it must first make a TN2 Mind + Sharp Senses goal roll to succeed. This Mind roll is a free action.

Models in active hiding cannot be charged unless the would-be charger wins an opposed Mind vs. Agility contest. This Mind roll is a free action. A model that fails to detect an intended target cannot charge it, and may instead choose to charge another foe, or do something else.

Interrupted Charges

When a model with a held action (see below) interrupts a charging model by moving into base contact, the charging model may choose to resolve its charge against the interrupting model, or if it survives the attack, break away and continue its charge against its original target. If the interrupting model is counter-charging, both models get their charge bonus (see Held Actions, pg. 11 for more on this).

Difficult Ground

Muddy fields, shallow water, and uneven terrain can slow a model down. Models moving through areas designated as difficult

Combat and Movement

ground move only 1" for every 2" of their Move value spent.

Models charging through difficult ground do not receive the normal charge bonus unless their last 3" of movement before they make base contact are in clear terrain.

FREE ACTIONS
Free actions require little time to complete and usually involve the model trying to quickly sense its surroundings. There are two major types of Free Actions.

Perception Checks
Most perception checks using the Mind attribute are free actions. A model may perform a number of free actions equal to its Mind attribute. A perception check most often occurs when a model is trying to spot a hidden or out of sight model.

Dropping Prone
At any time during its turn a model may drop prone as a free action. Dropping Prone immediately ends any charge action, but normal move actions may continue at a crawling pace (see Crawling below).

SPECIAL ACTIONS
These are actions that cover a wide array of options on the tabletop.

Climbing
Buildings and walls outfitted with stairs and ladders are treated normally for purposes of calculating distance moved. Climbing a surface without stairs or ladders is a special kind of Movement that halves the model's Move value. A model may not Charge up a vertical surface, and must stop at its base and wait until next turn to begin its ascent.

Crawling
Crawling is a type of movement that may occur after a model drops prone or is knocked down. A model crawls half its Move score, or if it drops prone in the course of normal movement, half its remaining Move score.

Falling
Not really an action, falling often results in injury. The DN of a fall is equal to one plus one for every full 2" the model falls. Falls of 1" or less are ignored. Models who survive a fall begin their next turn knocked down, and must spend 2" of their Move value to stand up.

Example: *Mladic falls 8" from a castle battlement. When he hits the ground he rolls his DR versus DN5 (1 + 4).*

Forcing Doors
Models may use a special action to attempt to force open a locked or stuck door. Depending on the scenario or situation, a locked or stuck door will have a TN assigned to it that reflects the difficulty in breaking it down. Models wishing to force such a door open must make a Strength goal roll and match or exceed the door's TN. If they exceed the TN by 2+ goals the door is shattered. Certain special traits allow models to burst through doors without making this roll. See the Special Traits section in Chapter V for more details.

If the scenario dictates that it is permissible, it requires a special action for a model to bar or block a door, and this must be done while within 1" of the door.

A standard wooden door to the room of an inn or hostel might have TN2, while a reinforced door in a keep or castle might have TN3 or even TN4. Prison doors could easily reach TN4 or TN5.

Held Actions
In the card-based Initiative system, a model may hold its action by holding its card, using it later in the round to act when it sees fit. This is a free action. In the dice-based Initiative system, a model may be activated then use a free action to hold.

If this held action would interrupt the action of another model, the two models should make Opposed Agility goal rolls, with the winner taking his action. Ties go to the model with the held action. If a model with a held action is holding a Joker card, it may interrupt

Combat and Movement

automatically with no opposed roll. Held actions may not carry over to the next round.

The model with the held action may decide exactly when to interrupt the acting model if it wins the opposed contest. This comes into play in situations where a model wants to maximize his weapon's effective range or avoid the negative effects of special traits like Terrifying Aura.

However, the interrupting model may still not pre-measure, but as the opposing player moves his model he can make his best guess about when the optimal time to interrupt is and announce it.

Models interrupted by a model with a held action may finish their actions once the interrupting model has completed its turn. An interrupted model directly affected by a model with a held action (i.e., attacked) may resume its turn once the interrupting model has completed its attacks (provided it is still able).

Example: *Hampton is moving down a steep mountain pass when a group of Gypsies with a held action charges him. If Hampton survives their attack, he can continue his movement, or alternately, remain locked in combat with the robbers and take a few licks at them.*

Jumping
A model that wishes to jump a chasm or vault an obstacle makes a Strength goal roll. A model can jump 2" horizontally and 1" vertically for every goal rolled. For normal human models this distance cannot exceed the model's total move value, and vertical jumps may never exceed 2".

Jumps totaling less than the model's Move value cost the model that much of its movement for its turn. For example, a model with 5" Move jumps a 3" chasm, and can then move a total of 2" more that turn. Horizontal jumps may be combined with the Charge action, but may not exceed the model's total move + charge allowance for its turn.

Through the course of its charge a model may attempt to make vertical leaps over any number of intervening obstacles. This requires the normal jumping goal roll outlined above, but if the model fails a jump its movement for that round ends.

Players may not pre-measure the distance needed to jump a chasm or vault an obstacle. Instead the intention to jump is announced, then the distance is measured and the Strength goal roll is made. Models that do not score enough goals to make the jump over a chasm fall.

Knocked Down/Standing Up
Models in CIC will sometimes find themselves knocked down for one reason or another. Models that are knocked down must spend 2" of their Move action to stand up. A model that has been knocked down may not charge the turn it gets up.

Models attacking a knocked down model enjoy +1D to close combat attacks. Knocked down or crawling models enjoy +1D to their defense goal rolls against ranged attacks.

Hiding
A model that ends its turn in some sort of cover may choose to hide as a special action. A hiding model cannot be Charged or targeted by ranged attacks unless the potential attacker wins an opposed Mind vs. Agility contest with the hiding model. Once a model chooses to hide, its turn has ended. Attempting to spot a hidden model counts as a free action. Models hiding in hard cover receive +2D to this contest, and models hiding in soft cover receive +1D.

Use Item/Pick-up Object
This is a catchall action category that allows models to interact with terrain objectives and objects in the field of play. Some scenarios may call for the use/activation of a particular item (artifact, medical kit, etc.), which could involve a Mind or Agility check.

Picking up an item always counts as a special action unless a scenario dictates otherwise.

Combat and Movement

Using an item can either be a free action or special action, usually as the scenario dictates.

Some scenarios may call for the freeing of a prisoner, or the recovery of some object (an ancient tome, magical weapon, etc.). Some of these actions require goal rolls, and some require only the expenditure of a special action. The requirements of specific actions in this category will be covered in the relevant scenario descriptions (see Chapter VII: Campaigns).

COMBAT

There are two types of combat in Chaos in Carpathia, close combat and ranged combat. Both involve opposed goal rolls. A model may expend its Combat action to do one of the two, but not both.

Choosing Targets

When choosing whom to attack, a model may target any enemy model it desires, whether they are at range or in close combat.

Combat and Movement

CLOSE COMBAT

Close Combat in CIC requires combatants to be in base contact. Models may move normally into close combat and expend their Combat action to attack, or combine their move with a combat action into a charge. Models that charge into close combat attack at +2 dice to their Agility.

The attacking model in close combat rolls its Agility attribute (plus Special Traits or situational modifiers) vs. the defender's Agility attribute (plus Special Traits or situational modifiers), if the attacker gets more goals than the defender, he has hit, and additional goals can add to the effectiveness of his attack in the next phase of combat resolution.

If the defender ties or gets more goals than the attacker, she has fought him off. An attacker who moved normally (i.e., did not charge) into close combat can use its attack action as normal, but does not gain the benefits of charging.

Example: *Hampton and a devilish cult leader are battling in some haunted ruin in the countryside. It's Hampton's turn and he has just charged into close combat with the cult leader. Hampton rolls his Agility 3 plus two extra dice for the charge, for a total of five dice. He gets 2, 4, 4, 5, and 6 for five goals. The Cult Leader rolls 2, 3, and 5 for one goal. Hampton wins the contest 5 goals to 1, and the players now move on to the damage phase of the combat resolution.*

DAMAGE IN CLOSE COMBAT

Damage rolls in close combat match the weapon or attack's damage number against the target's damage resistance (referred to hereafter as DR) roll. The attacker's damage number may be enhanced by a particularly effective attack. If the attacker beats the defender by 3+ goals, the attacker adds +1 to his damage number.

Additionally, if the attacker possesses Strength of 4 or greater it adds an additional +1 to the attack's DN. This +1 for Strength is already factored into any natural attacks in the model profiles in the warband section presented later in this book.

The equipment section presented later lists DN's for various weapons and attacks. A model attacking a foe barehanded has DN2 (+1 if it possesses Strength 4+).

The target model's DR consists of 1 + its Strength, plus any dice gained from Special Traits, equipment and/or situational factors. The defender rolls his DR against the attack's damage number, and if he meets or exceeds this number he takes no damage. If the defender fails this roll the number he fails by equals the amount of Vitality inflicted by that attack.

Example: *Hampton has just struck the cult leader with a knife slash, and now it's time to resolve the damage. The damage number for Hampton's knife attack is a base of 4, plus one for the four goals he beat his foe by in the previous example, making the total number equal to 5.*

The cult leader has Strength 3, so his DR is 4 dice (1 + 3). He rolls his resistance and gets 1, 4, 4 and 5 for three goals. The cult leader fails to match the attack's damage number, losing by 2 goals, and thus loses two Vitality points.

BREAKING FROM CLOSE COMBAT

A model can move or charge away from close combat, but his opponent can launch an immediate, free attack on the escaping model. This attack is still opposed, as it is assumed that the model breaking from combat is making a fighting withdrawal from combat. If he's fighting multiple opponents, each one gets a free attack. Even if the model breaking from combat takes Vitality loss, it can still get away as long as it does not lose its last Vitality point.

If a model attacks and damages a foe, then breaks from close combat that same round, the foe damaged by its attack does not get the normal free attack on the model breaking from combat.

MULTIPLE FOES IN CLOSE COMBAT

Models ganging-up on a single defender gain a number of bonus attack and defense dice equal to their numerical advantage. If two models were attacking one model, each of the attacking models would gain +1 die to their Agility attribute for the attack. If on a later turn, a third model rushed in, all three allied models would gain +2 dice to their attacks for the three-to-one advantage. Models with a numerical advantage in close combat may break away without suffering the normal penalty for breaking from close combat. Models may not enjoy more than a +5 bonus from friends in close combat.

Each henchmen group aiding character models in close combat provide the equivalent of +1 die worth of friends.

AID IN CLOSE COMBAT

When a friendly model rushes in to help a teammate assailed by multiple foes, it engages one of the enemy models, and a separate close combat ensues. Keeping them in base contact, move the two models 1" away from the original close combat.

Example: *Heroine Patricia Kincaid is battling Mladic the Blood Servant and his partner. Not liking those odds, Kincaid's comrade, Hampton, charges Mladic. Mladic and Hampton break off into their own, separate close combat 1" away, while Kincaid and the remaining thug continue to battle.*

A NOTE ON LEAVING CLOSE COMBAT

Once a model leaves a close combat during its turn it may not re-enter that same close combat later in the turn. It may enter another combat or perform some other action as the rules allow.

KNOCKED-DOWN MODELS

Models that are knocked down are more vulnerable to attack, and models in close combat against them receive a +1 die bonus on the attack goal roll.

RANGED COMBAT

Ranged combat in CIC occurs when a model attacks another model from a distance. Models use their Agility attribute as the basis for the ranged attack, adding in dice from any special traits they might possess. Defending models oppose attackers with their Agility attribute, also adding in dice from any special traits they might possess.

If the attacker rolls more goals than the defender, the shot results in a hit. The defender must then make a damage resistance goal roll versus the attack's DN# (just as described in close combat above). Just as in close combat, the attacker adds +1 to the DN of the attack if he beat his target by 3+ goals.

Example: *A brigand fires his rifle at a fleeing treasure hunter. He rolls his attack and scores 4 goals on the throw, and the treasure hunter rolls her Agility and gets 1 goal for defense. The brigand has hit, and moves on to damage, adding +1 to his rifle's DN.*

Just as in close combat, models struck in range combat roll their DR versus the attack's DN. If they match or exceed the DN, they take no damage, but if they fail, they suffer the difference in Vitality loss.

Damage from ranged attacks against henchmen is resolved slightly differently than with character models. This is covered in Chapter III: Henchmen.

RANGED ATTACKS IN CLOSE COMBAT

Ranged Attacks may not be made in close combat. Models in base contact with enemy

Combat and Movement

models must leave combat in order to make ranged attacks. See Breaking From Close Combat above for more information on this.

SEEING TARGETS

A model must be able to see at least some part of its target to hit it with a ranged attack. If the attacking model cannot draw a straight, uninterrupted line to its target, it may not fire. Friendly models do not block line of site, but enemy models do.

ATTACK RANGES

Most ranged attacks in Chaos in Carpathia, whether gun shots or magical blasts, have an Effective Range (ER) and Maximum Range (MR). All attacks with a weapon or special trait within its ER are standard opposed actions. When an attacker goes beyond his weapon or trait's ER, his target gains +2 dice to its defense roll. An attacking model cannot attempt a shot that exceeds twice his weapon or attack's ER; this is the weapon or attack's Maximum Range (MR).

Example: *A German policeman's pistol is a ranged attack with an ER of 8". He can shoot at targets out to 8" with no penalty. His MR is 16", and attacks between 9" - 16" will grant targets a +2 dice defense bonus. The German's pistol cannot reach targets beyond 16".*

DARKNESS

These rules assume most battles take place at night or underground. It is this assumption that drives the decision to make weapon ranges rather short compared to some other skirmish games. Players will find that certain scenarios and special events create circumstances of even greater darkness, and in these cases special rules will apply. In all other cases it is assumed models possess sufficient illumination to move, fight, and try to achieve their goals on the tabletop.

COVER

There are two types of cover in CIC, hard and soft. Hard cover is any substance with stopping power like a ship's bulkhead, cave wall, or hoffbrau table. Soft cover is a less durable form of cover that still might spoil an attacker's aim or deflect a shot. Examples of soft cover include hedges, bystanders, or drapery.

Models in hard cover receive +2 dice to their defense rolls.

Models in soft cover receive +1 die to their defense rolls.

As models in CIC are thought to be in constant motion, a model need only be partially obscured by the cover to receive its full benefits. If even just a leg or arm is obscured, the model is in cover!

STACKING MODIFIERS

Modifiers for ranged combat stack. For instance, if the German policeman fires on a target standing in soft cover 15" away, his target would have a +3 dice bonus to its defense roll for the shot (+1 die from the soft cover and +2 dice for exceeding his ER of 8").

RADIUS ATTACKS

Certain ranged attacks (shotgun blasts, bombs, gas, etc.) cover a wider area than normal. A radius attack affects a certain area in inches from the center of the original target, possibly affecting adjacent models. If even a portion of an adjacent model's base is touched by the radius attack, that model must also make an opposed defense roll against the same attack roll as the original target.

Example: *A farmer fires his Shotgun (2" Radius) at a trio of Blood Servants moving toward him down a narrow corridor. The first Blood Servant is the primary target, and the second Blood Servant 1" behind him is also caught in the blast, while the third model standing 2" behind the second does not have to make a defense roll.*

FIRING INTO CLOSE COMBAT

Models can fire ranged attacks into close

combat. Their targets make an opposed Agility roll just as in a normal ranged attack, but add +1 die to their defense due to the swirling nature of the action. If the firing model misses, there is a chance that the other models in the close combat could be hit by the attack.

Assign each additional model in the close combat a number between one and six, and then roll a D6. If a model's number is rolled, it is hit by the errant attack, and must make an opposed damage resistance goal roll versus the basic DN of the attack. If no model's number is rolled, the shot simply misses as normal.

its last Vitality box marked off, it must make a TN3 Resolve check to remain standing. Certain special traits may increase this KO TN. See Chapter V: Special Traits for more details.

If the model fails this check it is placed face down on the table where it last stood. Unless a comrade can apply first aid or magical healing to it, the model is effectively out of the battle.

If the model makes its KO check, it can remain standing and fight as normal. However, if it sustains any further Vitality loss, it is KO'ed with no further Resolve checks. The model is placed face down to await its fate.

MORE ON DAMAGE

Every model in CIC has a Vitality rating tracked using circles along the bottom of its Stat Profile. A model always begins every one-off battle at its peak Vitality (usually 3 for Characters). Models involved in a Campaign can sustain injuries that carry over from battle to battle. Vitality is lost whenever a model is hit and then fails to match the attack's DN.

Certain attacks are so powerful that they can do greater damage no matter where they hit. These attacks (usually specific types of weapons) add +1 to their base DN when they beat the opponent's defense goal roll by 2+ goals instead of the normal 3+ goals.

Vitality is marked off moving from left to right on the track.

KO CHECKS

When a character marks off its last box in the Vitality track this forces a KO check. KO is short for Knockout, and when a model has

Example: *Aga the Turk suffers a gun shot from a foe and rolls his DR pool versus a TN5 damage number. Aga's player rolls poorly, getting only 2 goals. Aga suffers the difference of three in Vitality loss. He started the game with 3 Vitality, so this shot takes him to zero! Aga's player rolls his Resolve 4 versus the normal TN3 and scores only 2 goals. Aga is KO'ed!*

COUP DE GRACE

KO'ed models are at the mercy of their enemies. An enemy model in base contact with a KO'ed foe can elect to spend its combat action and deliver a Coup de Grace blow that removes the model from the table. No roll is necessary as the KO'ed model is utterly defenseless. A model that is in base contact with both a KO'ed and a fully functioning enemy model cannot deliver a Coup de Grace as it must fully concentrate on battling the more dangerous foe.

Models may perform a ranged Coup de Grace by spending their combat action and making a TN3 Ranged Attack goal roll.

Combat and Movement

BURNING

Models struck by torches or otherwise surrounded by flame suffer a chance of catching fire. Models struck by a torch catch fire on a 5+ D6 roll. Once aflame, a model suffers a DN3 hit each round when it takes its turn. This damage is resisted at the beginning of the model's turn, before any other actions are resolved. A model may use a special action to put itself out. This requires only the expenditure of the special action and succeeds automatically.

WEAPONS

Models in CIC will often use ranged or close combat weapons. If a model has a weapon on its profile, it is assumed to be able to produce and use that weapon as a free action. For example, if Count Zoltan possesses both a revolver and a sword, he can use either during the course of his turn by switching from one to another as a free action.

Players should keep in mind which weapon their model is currently wielding, as the number of free actions a model possesses is limited by its Mind, and switching back and forth will quickly exhaust them.

COMBAT MANUEVERS

Heroic combat is all about cinematic, action-packed fight scenes involving dynamic leaps, whirlwind attacks, and improbable maneuvers. The following maneuvers allow models on the tabletop to simulate that kind of fast-paced, dynamic action. Each maneuver counts as a Combat action. Each maneuver is presented with its name and rule description. Players and fans of the genre are encouraged to develop new maneuvers of their own, although all players should agree upon a maneuver's rules before it is used in a game.

AIMED SHOT

Character models attempting Agility-based ranged attacks can sacrifice some of their movement to make an Aimed Shot. A model that moves 2" or less may declare that it is making an Aimed Shot. Aimed Shots add +1 die to the character model's attack goal roll. Henchmen groups may not use this maneuver.

DISARM

If an attacker declares a disarm attempt before rolling the dice, he makes a close combat attack as normal, but if he hits he causes no damage. Instead the attacker and defender make opposed Agility or Strength (each chooses his best) goals rolls. If the attacker wins, he has successfully knocked one of his foe's weapons (attacker's choice) from his person. The weapon lands in a random direction 1" away from the model, and may be retrieved as a Special Action. Disarms may be attempted at the end of a Charge. Disarms may not be attempted against Henchmen groups.

Disarms may also be used to relieve models of certain scenario objectives they are carrying around with them. Unless the target model has used a special action to secure the scenario objective in a pouch or sack, the object is a suitable target for this maneuver.

Lost weapons are always recovered at the end of the game.

TRIP

A Trip maneuver is an attack that does no damage, but if it succeeds, knocks the opponent down (see the rules for Knocked Down models above). Models attempting a Trip with a spear, staff or other pole-type weapon (see the Weapons section below) receive +1D to their attack goal rolls. Models that are tripped within 1" of the edge of a sheer drop could fall, and must make a TN2 Agility goal roll to avoid falling. This maneuver may only be used for close combat attacks.

~3~

Henchmen

NOTES ON HENCHMEN

ENCHMEN GROUPS IN CIC WORK A LITTLE DIFFERENTLY than normal characters. Although a henchmen group can contain anywhere between 5 - 20 models, it functions as a single model on the tabletop, fighting, moving, and attacking as one.

GROUPING

Henchmen must remain close to each other during the course of a battle. Each model in the group must be within 2" of another member of the group. They may move in a line, or as a looser formation, but this 2" limit must be maintained. Since Vitality loss against henchmen groups results in the removal of members of the group, casualties should be removed in such a way as to preserve group integrity whenever possible.

CLOSE COMBAT

No matter their number, Henchmen Groups make only one attack goal roll in close combat, but do enjoy the benefits of having multiple friends.

Unlike character models, all henchmen in a group do not have to be in base contact for the group to enjoy the friends in close combat bonus. If a character or henchmen group charges and makes contact with at least one model in a henchmen group, the entire group is considered to be in the combat. For purposes of clarity, once a charge is completed against a henchmen group, move as many of the henchmen as practical into base contact with the charging model or models.

Henchmen groups receive +1 die to Agility for close combat attacks for every two members, up to a maximum of +5. No matter the henchmen group's size, it can never gain a bonus higher than +5 dice from multiple friends in close combat; this includes any dice from friendly character models.

Henchmen

Example: *Five cultists have charged Hampton and make one attack goal roll at +2 dice for their superior numbers. They would also receive +2 dice for the normal charge bonus.*

BREAKING AWAY

A lone henchmen group always suffers a free attack when breaking from close combat.

HENCHMEN AGAINST MULTIPLE FOES

When a friend rushes in to help in close combat against a Henchmen Group, simply split the henchmen group's members evenly across the enemy models, and add up bonuses accordingly. In the case of odd numbered Henchmen groups, the controlling player decides which foe gets the extra model.

These split henchmen groups fight as if they were separate groups, each with full actions, equipment, and special traits. Henchmen groups that are split in these instances still make Pinning checks (see below for more on Pinning) as one group.

If a split group that is more than 2" from the rest of its comrades KO's a foe in close combat, they must use their next available move action to rejoin the rest of their fellows. Any movement they expend to do this counts against the total movement of the group for that turn.

Example: *Caroline Pickard rushes in to close combat to aid her comrade, Hampton, who has been besieged by five Cossacks. Both Hampton and Pickard get two Cossacks apiece, and the Henchmen Group's player assigns the third one to Pickard.*

In the ensuing combat, the 3 Cossacks and Pickard wind up 3" away from Hampton's tussle with the other part of the henchmen group. The savage Cossacks manage to KO Pickard, while Hampton fights on with his group. Since the group battling Pickard finds itself 3" away from its fellows, they must use at least 1" of movement to regain their normal cohesion.

The group then finishes off Hampton and wants to move. They would get 4" of Move value instead of the normal 5" because of the 1" spent to reform.

HENCHMEN AND MULTIPLE FOES II

When a henchmen group and a character model outnumber a single foe and an enemy model rushes in to help by attacking the henchmen, the entire group is pulled away into a separate combat, leaving the two character models to battle each other.

Example: *A werewolf and a pack of wolves are locked in combat with a lone monster hunter. In the next round, a second monster hunter charges the pack of wolves. The second monster hunter and the entire pack of wolves are moved 1" away into their own separate combat. The lone werewolf and the original monster hunter are left to fight on against each other.*

HENCHMEN IN RANGED COMBAT

Henchmen in ranged combat make only one attack goal roll. Henchmen groups purchase ranged weapons just as character models, but they need pay the cost for the weapon only once. Due to their numbers, Henchmen have access to a special maneuver called Concentrated Fire. Henchmen groups with four or more members that move 2" or less may make a ranged attack that grants them +2 dice to Agility.

HENCHMEN AND DAMAGE

A Henchmen Group's Vitality rating is based on their numbers. A group of seven Gypsy bandits can take seven "hits" or points of Vitality loss in close combat. In cases where the removal of a particular henchmen model might be important, the player who controls the henchmen group decides which model is removed.

Henchmen

The exception to this rule occurs when henchmen sustain damage from ranged attacks. Unless a ranged weapon has some area effect (called Radius in the weapons section), it may only ever take one henchmen model out of action. Any remaining vitality point loss has a chance to Pin the remaining henchmen.

PINNING

When a henchmen group loses a model from ranged attacks, it may be pinned as a result. The henchmen group must make a Resolve check with a TN equal to 1 + the amount of extra vitality loss it would have suffered had it been a character model. A group that fails this check counts as being Pinned, suffering -2" to its Move value on its next turn, and granting foes +1 die to attack and defense goal rolls until the pinning effect clears at the end of their next turn. Pinning effects clear, or go away, automatically at the end of the henchmen group's next turn.

Pinned henchmen groups may not benefit from concentrated fire, or conduct other combat maneuvers.

Henchmen groups receive +1 die to their pinning checks for every two models remaining in the group, and may also add traits like Iron Will to the roll.

MULTIPLE PINS

A henchmen group may be pinned multiple times. The effects of multiple pins stack, so that a group that has been pinned twice would suffer -4" Move and grant foes +2 dice to attack and defense goal rolls. Multiple pins still clear, or go away, at the same time-the end of the henchmen group's next turn following being pinned.

Example: *A group of Cossack henchmen is struck by gunfire from an opposing character. The shot does 3 Vitality points of damage, but since the Cossacks are henchmen, only one model is removed, and the whole group makes a TN3 pinning check. The Cossacks fail their check and suffer a pin; until the end of their next turn they will be at -2" Move and their foes will enjoy +1 die attack and defense against them.*

~4~

Warbands

IN THIS SECTION PLAYERS WILL FIND WARBAND SELECTION LISTS for the various factions in CIC. Each list contains a number of options for warriors, occultists, explorers, monsters, and servants. Certain lists may contain limits on the numbers of certain model types. Unless otherwise noted, players may not mix and match character or henchmen groups from different warband rosters. Each player receives 325 pounds (GBP) to recruit and outfit his warband.

Every warband list also includes notes on equipment, including any extra costs a player must pay to outfit the models with each piece of equipment. These notes may also contain limitations on which models may be outfitted with certain pieces of equipment. Note: Most human models receive a knife or basic hand weapon for free, and this is indicated on their starting profile.

Following the warband lists is a roster of special and named characters suitable for inclusion in a number of warbands. Chapters V and VI list rules and explanations for Special Traits and Equipment (including weapons).

Players who exhaust their starting funds can add new warband members to their group by playing campaign games and earning resources. New members may be added from the starting list profiles below, or from the special characters list following the basic warband descriptions. For more on campaigns and how they work, players should see Chapter VII: Campaigns later in this book.

Note: Any listed close combat DN's for models with Strength of 4 or greater already reflect the +1 increase (see the Weapons section in Chapter VI: Equipment for more details).

Warbands - Monster Hunters

WESTERN EUROPEAN MONSTER HUNTERS

These men and women represent the best and brightest Europe has to offer in her struggle against the unholy monsters who threaten the very fate of the civilized world. Brought together from disparate backgrounds, these intrepid heroes and heroines overcome their fear to face the horrors of the Nameless Ones and the creatures of the savage wilderness.

Warband Trait: Well-Connected. This warband's close ties to normal human society give them an edge in resource gathering during the Upkeep phase of a campaign (see Chapter VII for more details). They receive +5 GBP provided they have at least one model who was not KO'ed during the previous battle.

Warband Trait: Combat Specialist. At the beginning of a campaign, or before a one-off battle, players may choose one model in this warband and shift its levels in Combat Attack, Combat Evade, Crack Shot and Iron Will as they see fit. No trait may be raised beyond 3 levels using this option, and a model may not possess more than one trait at 3 levels. This option may be used to give a model levels in trait it did not originally possess on its profile, or remove existing traits all together.

INTREPID LEADER (MANDATORY, 43 GBP)

Str	Agl	Mnd	Res	Move	DR Pool	Fate	Vitality
3	3	3	4	5"	4	4	3

This square-jawed hero often finds himself the unlikely leader of a band of motley adventurers. Usually young and fit, the Intrepid Leader surrounds himself with experts and skilled fighters, and although, brash, will still heed the advice of a more expert fighter. Some Intrepid Leaders begin their careers later in life, perhaps after a time as a soldier or explorer.

Special Traits
Combat Attack x 2
Combat Evade x 1
Crack Shot x 2
Dodge!
Iron Will x 1
Leader x 2

Equipment
Knife (DN4)

LEARNED SCHOLAR (MAX 1, 35 GBP)

Str	Agl	Mnd	Res	Move	DR Pool	Fate	Vitality
2	2	4	4	5"	3	4	3

Professor, elder, globe-trotting traveler, the learned scholar possesses encyclopedic knowledge of the world and its inhabitants, including the supernatural and monstrous ones. Although a liability in combat, Learned Scholars can sometimes tip the balance in special situations.

Special Traits
Combat Evade x 1
Crack Shot x 1
Iron Will x 2
Scholar x 3

Equipment
Truncheon (DN3)

Warbands - Monster Hunters

SLAYER (MAX 2, 40 GBP)

Str	Agl	Mnd	Res	Move	DR Pool	Fate	Vitality
4	3	2	3	5"	5[1]	3	3

These hardened fighters know only one desire: kill monsters. Whether witnessing a family member murdered at a young age or having suffered some other attack at the hands of the supernatural, a slayer's prowess is fueled by his or her hate. This singular passion sometimes makes them difficult comrades, as they can be heedless of the value of teamwork in battle.

Special Traits
Combat Attack x 3
Combat Evade x 1
Crack Shot x 2
Sharp Senses x 2
Solitary
Tough

Equipment
Knife (DN4)

RELIABLE MAN OR WOMAN (35 GBP)

Str	Agl	Mnd	Res	Move	DR Pool	Fate	Vitality
3	3	2	3	5"	4	3	3

The reliable man or woman provides extra muscle for the warband. Reliable men and women come from the ranks of the working class, and usually function as retainers for one of the more prominent members of the warband.

Special Traits
Combat Attack x 2
Combat Evade x 1
Crack Shot x 1
Sharp Senses x 1

Equipment
Knife (DN4)

HOLY MAN (OR WOMAN!) (MAX 1, 39 GBP)

Str	Agl	Mnd	Res	Move	DR Pool	Fate	Vitality
2	3	3	4	5"	3	4	3

Priests, nuns, clerics-these battlers of evil come in many stripes, but share a common belief in the True Faith. Their very presence can bolster a group of monster hunters and strike fear into the dark hearts of enemy monsters.

Special Traits
Combat Evade x 1
[] Inspiration
Iron Will x 1
Sharp Senses x 1
True Faith

Equipment
Holy Symbol

Warbands - Monster Hunters

THE AUTHORITIES (MAX 2, 41 GBP)

Str	Agl	Mnd	Res	Move	DR Pool	Fate	Vitality
3	2	2	3	5"	3	3	henchmen (5 members)

London Bobbies, Texas Rangers, Italian Polizi, no matter where they hail from, these brave souls are the nameless embodiment of law and order. They bravely step in to aid heroes when facing the minions of darkness, and often pay for it with their lives.

Special Traits
Combat Attack x 1
Combat Evade x 1
Crack Shot x 2
Sharp Senses x 1

Equipment
Truncheon
(DN3)

EXTRA MANPOWER

Players may add additional agents to a starting group at the cost of +3 GBP per agent. Players may add up to five additional models in this fashion.

WHY WE FIGHT THEM

The Vampires
"They are the lords of darkness, as immune to time as they are indignant to God's will. We hunt them because they hunt us. We slay them lest they slay us."

The Werewolves
"They represent nature unbound. Was it not God who said man must have dominion over the beasts? For man to prosper in the wild places of this world they must be rooted out. Still, they've no use for the blood-suckers, and that is one thing in their favor."

The Treasure Hunters
"Greed is sometimes more monstrous than any creature of the night. It drives these men, little more than dirty brigands, they are. If they cross us in our appointed task, we will see to it they receive their just rewards. The devil needs diggers in his hellish mines, and we will not hesitate to send them there."

VAMPIRE AND MINIONS

These princes of the night owe their existence (and their curse of eternal bloodlust) to the Nameless Ones. They walk in shadow playing games with the mortal world and its inhabitants as their pawns. Immortal and hard to kill, powerful vampires often attract a coterie of lesser blood-drinkers and human scum to do their bidding.

They are as wont to battle each other as they are the humans they prey upon, and they hate the werewolves with great fervor.

Note: Players wishing to run Vampire warbands should choose either a Nosferatu or Romanian vampire to lead their bands. Players may not have both types in a single band.

NOSFERATU (MANDATORY, 56 GBP)

Str	Agl	Mnd	Res	Move	DR Pool	Fate	Vitality
5	4	3	5	6"	6 [3]*	5	3

This fearsome, pale, and gangly vampire relies on razor sharp claws and wiry strength to win his battles.

Special Traits
Combat Attack x 2
Combat Evade x 1
Claws (DN5)
Sharp Senses x 2
Vampire
[ ] [ ] [ ] Vampiric Might

Equipment
None (a Nosferatu may not use equipment or weapons)

* Re-rolls vs. Firearms only.

ROMANIAN VAMPIRE (MANDATORY, 72 GBP)

Str	Agl	Mnd	Res	Move	DR Pool	Fate	Vitality
5	4	4	5	6"	6 [3]*	5	4

This vampire's handsome countenance and aristocratic bearing belie the beast within him. He is capable of acts of savagery every bit as terrible as his Nosferatu "cousin."

Special Traits
Combat Attack x 2
Combat Evade x 2
Claws (DN6)
Sharp Senses x 2
Vampire
[ ] [ ] Vampiric Might
[ ] Shape of the Bat
[ ] Shape of the Beast

Equipment
Romanian vampires may purchase a sword or dagger, but eschew the use of firearms or other ranged weapons.

* Re-rolls vs. Firearms only.

Vampire models may choose one of the following special traits, or an additional use of an existing trait at the listed additional cost:

- Terrifying Aura +8 GBP
- Wall-Crawler +5 GBP
- Mist Form +10 GBP
- Dodge +2 GBP
- Shape of the Bat (one use) +5 GBP
- Shape of the Beast (one use) +5 GBP

Warbands - Vampire and Minions

LESSER VAMPIRE (MAX 2, 60 GBP)

Str	Agl	Mnd	Res	Move	DR Pool	Fate	Vitality
4	4	3	4	6"	5 [3]*	4	3

These weaker vampires might be brides or consorts of the leader, or perhaps favored Blood Servants or minions finally brought over to the undead world.

* Re-rolls vs. Firearms only.

Special Traits
Combat Attack x 2
Combat Evade x 1
Claws (DN5)
Sharp Senses x 1
Vampire
[ ] [ ] Vampiric Might

Equipment
Lesser vampires may purchase a sword or dagger, but eschew the use of firearms or other ranged weapons.

BLOOD SERVANT (MAX 2, 36 PTS)

Str	Agl	Mnd	Res	Move	DR Pool	Fate	Vitality
4	3	2	3	5"	5	3	3

Vampires reward some loyal human servants by feeding them drops of their blood, extending their lives and giving them limited supernatural powers. These minions become Blood Servants and do their master's bidding during the daylight hours.

Special Traits
Combat Attack x 1
Crack Shot x 1
Sharp Senses x 1
[ ] Vampiric Might

Equipment
Knife (DN4)

COSSACK HERO (MAX 1, 36 PTS)

Str	Agl	Mnd	Res	Move	DR Pool	Fate	Vitality
4	3	2	3	5"	5[1]	3	3

Sometimes a particularly adept servant will rise from the ranks of a vampire's Cossack minions. This able fighter gains increased spoils and responsibilities in the band.

Special Traits
Combat Attack x 2
Crack Shot x 2
Tough

Equipment
Knife (DN4)

Warbands - Vampire and Minions

COSSACK GUARD (MAX 2, 35 GBP)

Str	Agl	Mnd	Res	Move	DR Pool	Fate	Vitality
3	3	2	3	5"	3	3	henchmen (5 members)

Powerful vampires often surround themselves with retinues of bonded humans. The fierce and resourceful Cossacks have been loyal vampire minions since the time of Dracula himself.

Special Traits
Combat Attack x 2
Crack Shot x 1
Sharp Senses x 1

Equipment
Knife (DN4)

Extra Cossacks
Players may add additional Cossacks to a starting group at the cost of +3 GBP per Cossack. Players may add up to five additional models in this fashion.

VAMPIRES AND EQUIPMENT

No member of the vampire warband may purchase holy symbols, garlic, or lucky charms. Only Cossacks and Blood Servants may purchase firearms.

WHY WE FIGHT THEM

The Monster Hunters

"Can they stop us? Do they think their pitiful faith in a dead god can save them? Our gods live within us, and we will unlock the doors that bind them to their domains and welcome them to ours. And the blood of the would-be slayers will be our key."

The Werewolves

"Pathetic dogs. We will bathe in their blood! We are the true hunters of the night, and we will own it and make it a welcome place for our Nameless masters."

The Treasure Hunters

"Fools. They think they can steal our secrets and the wealth we've amassed. Their blood will slake our thirst and strengthen us for future battles."

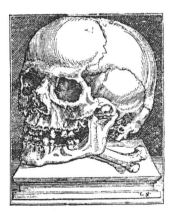

WEREWOLF PACK

Werewolf packs roam the wilds of old Europe and the British Isles preying upon unwary travelers and protecting their woodland domains. They normally consist of a Werewolf Pack Leader, Lesser Werewolves, and a number of normal wolves. If the situation arises, they can be moved to travel to seek some goal. They have as little love for vampires as they do normal humans, and they despise the unnatural powers of the Nameless Ones.

Warband note: The only special character willing to work with a Werewolf Pack is the Old Woodsman.

WEREWOLF PACK LEADER (MAX 1, 65 GBP)

Str	Agl	Mnd	Res	Move	DR Pool	Fate	Vitality
5	4	2	4	7"	6 [3]*	4	4

The pack Leader is the mightiest werewolf in his area, bringing together a number of lesser werewolves and regular wolves to his call. Some pack leaders are noble and direct their packs to prey upon only beasts and monsters, while others delight in slaying humans as readily as other creatures.

* No re-rolls vs. silver weapons.

Special Traits
Combat Attack x 3
Claws (DN6)
[] [] Killing Strike
Sharp Senses x 2
Werewolf

Equipment
Werewolves may not use equipment of any kind.

LESSER WEREWOLF (MAX 3, 55 GBP)

Str	Agl	Mnd	Res	Move	DR Pool	Fate	Vitality
5	3	2	3	7"	6 [3]*	3	3

Lesser werewolves are powerful foes beholden only to their pack leader. They possess all of his animal cunning and power in a slightly smaller package.

* No re-rolls vs. silver weapons.

Special Traits
Combat Attack x 3
Claws (DN6)
[] Killing Strike
Sharp Senses x 2
Werewolf

Equipment
Werewolves may not use equipment of any kind.

Werewolf Models may choose one of the following special traits at the listed additional cost:
- Speed Burst (one use) +3 GBP
- Terrifying Aura +8 GBP (pack leader only)
- Iron Will (+1D) +2 GBP

Warbands - Werewolf Pack

WOLF PACK (MAX 3, 52 GBP)

Str	Agl	Mnd	Res	Move	DR Pool	Fate	Vitality
3	3	1	2	8"	3	2	5 wolves

Wolf packs consist of normal wolves in servitude to the power of the Werewolf Pack Leader. Although they are part of the pack, normal wolves are often ill-used by their supernatural brethren, thrown into the fray to shield them from the terrible power of mankind's modern weapons. In their favor, normal wolves do not share the werewolf's vulnerability to silver.

Special Traits
Animal
Combat Attack x 2
Combat Evade x 1
Bite (DN5)
Sharp Senses x 3

Equipment
Wolves may not use equipment of any kind.

Enlarged Pack
Players may add additional wolves to a starting pack at the cost of +3 GBP per wolf.

ESCAPED ASYLUM INMATE (26 GBP, MAX 3)

Str	Agl	Mnd	Res	Move	DR Pool	Fate	Vitality
4	2	2	4	5"	5	4	3

These exiles from society have suffered greatly at the hands of rogue alienists and the public's general lack of understanding of their mental infirmities. This tortured existence has pushed them toward the wilder side of human nature, and given some of them an affinity for the raging beasts that inhabit the wild lands. At times those who escape will join the werewolves in a quest for vengeance, and the werewolves, sensing a kindred spirit, welcome them.

Special Traits
Animal
Combat Attack x 2
Inhuman Strength (DN4)

Equipment
Asylum patients may carry no equipment, although they may search for and carry scenario objectives.

WHY WE FIGHT THEM

The Monster Hunters
"Monsters? Who are the real monsters? They burn our woods, slay our children, drive away our prey. They stand in our way when we try to hunt the blood-drinkers. We must resist them to the end. Even if it means our deaths."

The Vampires
"These fiends would commune with the Nameless Ones and spread their foul taint around the world. While we breathe we hunt them."

The Treasure Hunters
"They trespass on our lands and foul the earth with their delving. When they stray into our lands they become prey."

TREASURE HUNTERS

Bands of treasure hunters roam the world attracted to ancient sites by the promise of wealth or power. Some wind up recruited into the secret battles for or against the supernatural threats that plague mankind. Unscrupulous bands of treasure hunters often find themselves in the employ of servants of the Nameless Ones. Others might walk a different path and oppose the growing evil of the elder gods.

Warband Trait: Well-Connected. This warband's close ties to normal human society give them an edge in resource gathering during the Upkeep phase of a campaign (see Chapter VII for more details). They receive +5 GBP provided they have at least one model who was not KO'ed during the previous battle.

Warband Trait: Combat Specialist. At the beginning of a campaign, or before a one-off battle, players may choose one model in this warband and shift its levels in Combat Attack, Combat Evade, Crack Shot and Iron Will as they see fit. No trait may be raised beyond 3 levels using this option, and a model may not possess more than one trait at 3 levels. This option may be used to give a model levels in trait it did not originally possess on its profile, or remove existing traits all together.

TREASURE HUNTER LEADER (MAX 1, 55 GBP)

Str	Agl	Mnd	Res	Move	DR Pool	Fate	Vitality
3	3	3	4	5"	4	4	3

The treasure hunter leader is both the bankroll and the impetus for his band. Perhaps he is a wealthy man bored with the life of privilege, or maybe he is a born explorer filled with the lust for adventure. A corrupted leader might have dealings with the Nameless Ones, even allowing their servants into his band.

Special Traits
Combat Attack x 1
Combat Evade x 1
Crack Shot x 2
Leader x 2
Resources
Scholar x 1
Sharp Senses x 1

Equipment
Knife (DN4)

ADVENTUROUS SCHOLAR (MAX 1, 38 GBP)

Str	Agl	Mnd	Res	Move	DR Pool	Fate	Vitality
2	2	4	4	5"	3	7	3

Where the leader is the bank roll and idea man of the warband, the adventurous scholar provides key knowledge that gives the hunters a hard target to strive toward reaching.

Special Traits
Combat Evade x 1
Crack Shot x 1
Gypsy's Luck
Iron Will x 2
Scholar x 3

Equipment
Knife (DN4)

Warbands - Treasure Hunters

TREASURE HUNTING THUG (MAX 3, 42 GBP)

Str	Agl	Mnd	Res	Move	DR Pool	Fate	Vitality
3	3	2	3	5"	4[1]	3	3

The treasure hunting thug provides the muscle for the warband. Thugs are often desperate men whose membership in the band represents their last chance in life. Hard-bitten fighters, treasure hunting thugs always follow the orders of the warband leaders, because that's where the money lies.

Special Traits
Combat Attack x 2
Combat Evade x 1
Crack Shot x 3
Sharp Senses x 1
Tough

Equipment
Knife (DN4)

LABOR GANG (MAX 2, 34)

Str	Agl	Mnd	Res	Move	DR Pool	Fate	Vitality
3	2	2	3	5"	3	3	Henchmen (5 models)

Labor gangs provide the muscle and sweat needed to properly excavate the target sites of the treasure hunting warband. The pay is better than most menial jobs, but the labor gang often doesn't take into account the grave danger such work can expose them to.

Special Traits
Combat Attack x 1
Combat Evade x 1
Pack Mule
Sharp Senses x 1

Equipment
Pick or Shovel (DN4)

Extra Workers

Players may add additional workers to a starting gang at the cost of +3 GBP per extra member. Players may add up to five additional models in this fashion.

WHY WE FIGHT THEM

The Monster Hunters
"Sanctimonious fools! They think they can stop the darkness? The wealth of the old world lies in the ground, and that money can buy plenty of gas lamps."

The Vampires
"Didn't think they existed until that time in Danova when Strauss shot that blood-drinker point-blank and it kept on coming.

It took everything we had to bring that one down. Of course, he was carrying over 300 GBP in jewelry. Made it worth the effort."

The Werewolves
"Occupational hazard, the dogs. One thing you never forget when heading on a dig into the backwoods is your silver shot. A little silver and a little luck are what you need against those monsters."

Warbands - Special Characters

SPECIAL CHARACTERS

Players may choose to hire special characters for their games. Some special characters are named personalities, while others represent archetypes that might not otherwise fit into one of the warband lists presented above.

Each special character is provided with complete stats and listed equipment, including weapons. Special Characters may not use additional weapons or equipment from other lists unless otherwise specified. A Special character has both a listed cost and a retainer cost. The listed cost is what is paid for the initial battle he is used, while the retainer represents the cost of keeping the character for further battles. The retainer is paid after each battle from the warband's treasury.

Special characters do not earn experience and do not progress as normal characters do. Their stats remain static. A special character may never be named as the leader of a warband.

Unique special characters are singular individuals and cannot appear more than once on the warband's roster sheet. Perhaps through the implacable machinations of the Nameless Ones, it is possible for a special character to appear in the same battle in different warbands.

ARNIM VON DRAKEN
Cost: 45 Retainer: 5

Str	Agl	Mnd	Res	Move	DR Pool	Fate	Vitality
5	3	4	4	5"	6	4	3

From the depths of time comes this foul harbinger of the Nameless Ones. Arnim von Draken was the one who tempted Dracula with the power of his foul gods, transforming him into the vampiric beast he is to this day. Arnim's foul gifts have kept him alive these last three centuries, and he still harbors plans to spread the vile teachings of his Nameless cults.

Special Traits
Combat Attack x 2
[ ] [ ] Horrific Gaze
Sharp Senses x 2
Tentacle Attack (DN5)
Unique

Equipment
None.

Arnim von Draken will not work with the Western European Monster Hunters. Arnim von Draken's retainer is -2 GBP when working for Treasure Hunter warbands.

Warbands - Special Characters

THE BRAVE DOCTOR
Cost: 36 Retainer: 4

Str	Agl	Mnd	Res	Move	DR Pool	Fate	Vitality
2	2	4	3	5"	3	6	3

Nothing can be a more valuable asset to a warband than a doctor. Well traveled, a man of letters and good breeding, a doctor's presence during a battle can mean the difference between life and death. Whether they seek knowledge, adventure, or absolution from some past failure, doctors often find more than they bargained for when they come into contact with the servants of the supernatural Nameless Ones.

Special Traits
Dodge!
Gypsy's Luck
Healer

Equipment
Medical Bag

Doctors will not work for werewolves or vampires.

CANINE COMPANION
Cost: 25 Retainer: 3

Str	Agl	Mnd	Res	Move	DR Pool	Fate	Vitality
3	3	1	3	6"	4	3	2

This loyal dog follows someone in the warband, and the group's members have become its pack. It will fight to the death to save its master and his comrades, and all it asks for in return is a pat on the head and a bit of kibble.

Special Traits
Animal
Bite (DN4)
Combat Attack x 1
Combat Evade x 1
Sharp Senses x 3

Equipment
None.

EASTERN EUROPEAN HOLY MAN
Cost: 39 Retainer: 4

Str	Agl	Mnd	Res	Move	DR Pool	Fate	Vitality
2	3	3	4	5"	3	4	3

A member of the great Orthodox faith of Eastern Europe, this fanatical cleric will work for a warband in need of God's guidance and protection. However, he will not work with any warband who has a regular Holy Man as a current member. Canonical and spiritual differences preclude his association with what he views as a faith that is a "rotten branch" on the great tree Christendom.

Special Traits
Combat Evade x 1
[] Inspiration
Iron Will x 1
Sharp Senses x 1
True Faith

Equipment
Club (DN3)
Holy Symbol

Note: Besides the restrictions listed above, this character will not work for Werewolf or Vampire warbands.

Warbands - Special Characters

GYPSY KNIFE-MAN
Cost: 42 Retainer: 4

Str	Agl	Mnd	Res	Move	DR Pool	Fate	Vitality
3	3	2	4	5"	4	4	3

A cunning and brutal fighter, the Gypsy Knife-Man will work for almost anyone if the price is right. Festooned with knives, he takes pride in his skill with blades, and can use them to strike with alarming speed and power.

Special Traits
Combat Attack x 3
Combat Evade x 2
Knife-Fighter
Sharp Senses x 1

Equipment
Knives
Throwing Knives

THE OLD WOODSMAN
Cost: 48 Retainer: 5

Str	Agl	Mnd	Res	Move	DR Pool	Fate	Vitality
3	3	3	4	5"	4	4	3

The Old Woodsman knows the wilderness of old Europe well, perhaps too well. He has lived so long amid the wild things that some say he has lost touch with reality. Still, among guides and trackers he knows no peer, and he can handle himself in a fight as well.

Special Traits
Combat Attack x 1
Crack Shot x 2
Guide (At the beginning of the game, after all models have been set up, any warband with a Woodsman may make a free move action with one of its models.)
Pathfinder (Ignores difficult ground in woodland terrain.)
Sharp Senses x 2

Equipment
Knife (DN4)
Rifle

Warbands - Special Characters

THE MAD DOCTOR
Cost: 37 Retainer: 4

Str	Agl	Mnd	Res	Move	DR Pool	Fate	Vitality
2	2	5	4	5"	3	4	3

Filled with a burning desire to create life, the mad doctor delved perhaps too deeply into the mysteries beyond the veil and the experience transformed him. Along the way he managed to breathe the spark of life into a form composed of a crazy patchwork of body-parts. Now the Mad Doctor and his powerful charge roam the lands seeking to further pierce the veil between life and death. The Mad Doctor may never work for Monster Hunter warbands.

Special Traits

Healer

The Monster (The Monster must be hired along with the Mad Doctor. If the Doctor ever perishes in post-battle, the Monster automatically leaves the warband and is removed from the campaign, never to be hired again.)

Scholar x 4

Unique

Equipment

Medical Bag

THE MONSTER
Cost: 26 Retainer: 3

Str	Agl	Mnd	Res	Move	DR Pool	Fate	Vitality
6	2	1	3	4"	7	3	3

A twisted, tragic amalgam of dead flesh, the Monster was given life by the Mad Doctor. Now he wanders Europe with him protecting him as he searches for even greater knowledge of life and death. The monster may never work for Monster Hunter warbands.

Special Traits

Combat Attack x 2

The Mad Doctor (The mad Doctor must be hired along with the Monster. If the Monster ever perishes in post-battle, the Mad Doctor automatically leaves the warband and is removed from the campaign, never to be hired again.)

Fears Fire (Models carrying torches count as having Terrifying Aura against the Monster.)

Death-Grip (DN5 Close Combat Attack)

Unkillable (As long as the Mad Doctor survives a battle, the Monster need never roll on any post-battle table.

Unique

Equipment

None.

Warbands - Special Characters

MANSERVANT
Cost: 30 Retainer: 3

Str	Agl	Mnd	Res	Move	DR Pool	Fate	Vitality
3	3	2	3	5"	4[1]	3	3

The manservant is a loyal retainer of one of the party's members. Whether that loyalty is motivated by love, fear, or another reason, the manservant is constantly by his master's side, ready to do his bidding at a moment's notice.

Options
At the cost of +10 GBP players may remove Cowardly and add a small pistol to the Manservant's profile.

Special Traits
Cowardly
Pack Mule
Tough
Solitary
Dedicated

Equipment
Club (DN3)

MENTALIST
Cost: 40 Retainer: 4

Str	Agl	Mnd	Res	Move	DR Pool	Fate	Vitality
2	2	4	4	5"	3	7	3

The Mentalist could be a Gypsy fortune teller, a mystic from the Far East, or a dabbler in the dark arts of the Nameless Ones. Whatever his training, he has attained acute mental powers beyond the grasp of most mortal men. He will work with any warband if he thinks it will further his occult research.

Special Traits
Gypsy's Luck
Scholar X 2
[] [] Augury
[] [] Mesmerize

Equipment
Knife (DN4)

Warbands - Special Characters

WESTERN GUNFIGHTER
Cost: 48 Retainer: 5

Str	Agl	Mnd	Res	Move	DR Pool	Fate	Vitality
3	4	2	3	5"	4	3	3

The Western Gunfighter is a man out of place, and maybe even out of time. Come from across the ocean to right wrongs or make his fortune, he's a six-gun for hire. If he lacks principles, he'll work for the monsters. If he's the strong, silent, honorable type, he'll throw his lot in with the good guys. Either way, he'll get paid.

Special Traits
Combat Attack x 1
Combat Evade x 1
Crack Shot x 3
Dodge!
Sharp Senses x 2
[ ] Shootist (Once per battle the Gunfighter may fire both his pistols at the same time, making two ranged combat attacks in a single combat action. Targets receive +1D to opposed Agility rolls to avoid this attack.)

Equipment
Knife (DN4)
Revolver
  (large caliber)
Revolver
  (small caliber)

~5~

Special Traits

SPECIAL TRAITS DEFINE THE UNIQUE and sometimes supernatural abilities possessed by models in Chaos in Carpathia.

ANIMAL

Animal models possess raw cunning but not human-level intelligence. They cannot search for scenario objectives (except where specified by specific scenario rules), use equipment, or perform complex special actions. Animals receive +2D on all jump checks.

AUGURY

This trait may be used a number of times indicated by the model's profile in the warband lists.

Models with this trait have ESP, premonitions, or are otherwise connected to other planes of existence. Using Augury counts as a free action, and allows the model to either take its turn immediately, without regard to normal turn order, or to add two dice to any check for a hidden model, trap, or scenario objective.

CLAWS

The model possesses claws which it uses to slash foes in close combat. The DN number of the claws is noted in each model's profile in

the warband lists, and if the model possesses Strength 4 or greater, this has already been factored into the final DN number presented there.

COMBAT ATTACK

A model's Combat Attack reflects it's training or sheer offensive ferocity in battle. Models add their rating in Combat Attack to their attack goal rolls in close combat.

COMBAT EVADE

A model's Combat Evade reflects its training or native elusiveness in close combat. Models add their rating in Combat Evade to their defense goal rolls in close combat.

COWARDLY

Cowardly characters must make Pinning checks whenever they suffer Vitality loss. Whenever a cowardly character suffers any vitality loss, he must make a TN3 Resolve goal roll or suffer pinning similar to henchmen groups. A pinned character suffers -2" Move and may not charge. Pinned characters remain pinned until the end of their next turn after suffering the damage that resulted in their being pinned.

CRACK SHOT

Dice in Crack Shot may be added to a model's attack Agility goal rolls in ranged combat.

DEDICATED

Models with this trait are unusually loyal to a particular model in the warband. This "master" model must be designated when the manservant is purchased. A dedicated model ignores effects of the Cowardly trait as long as his master is within 2". He also ignores the effects of Solitary if he is aiding or receiving aid from his master in combat.

If a master model is hit in close combat, a dedicated model within 2" may throw his body in the way to absorb the blow. The dedicated model will test against the DN of the successful attack with his own DR-1 (he can't effectively defend himself AND his master) and suffer all effects of the blow.

DODGE!

Models possessing this trait are shifty and tough to target with ranged attacks. Models with this trait add +1 die to their Agility defense goal rolls in ranged combat.

GYPSY'S LUCK

Lucky models with this trait begin the game with +3 Fate dice and as a free action may give their Fate dice to friendly models within 10" of them. These dice count as being used just as if the model had spent them on itself. Unlike normal models, their maximum Fate dice total is equal to three times their Resolve attribute.

HEALER

Models possessing this trait may use their medical or folk knowledge to heal injured and KO'ed models. The Healer model must make a Mind goal roll; every 2 goals scored restores 1 lost Vitality point to the model. A model may not benefit from more than one successful Healer roll per game. A Medical Kit adds dice to this roll (see the Equipment section). This trait may not be used to restore lost henchmen.

HORRIFIC GAZE

This trait may be used a number of times indicated by the model's profile in the warband lists. Models possessing this trait may make a 6" gaze attack pitting their Resolve + Iron Will against their target's Resolve + Iron Will. If the attacker succeeds the target suffers a DN4 hit that must be resisted by the target's Resolve + Iron Will. If the attacker succeeds by 3+ goals he adds +1 to the DN of the attack.

INSPIRATION

This trait may be used a number of times indicated by the model's profile in the warband lists. A model possessing this trait may use a free action to activate it. All friendly, non-Animal models within 5" of the inspiring model when the trait is activated receive +1 die to their next attack and defense goal rolls.

Example: *Brother Aquinus possesses Inspiration and when his turn begins he moves 5" then spends a free action to activate the trait. His comrades Carolina*

Special Traits

and Radu are both within 5" of him when he declares the use of the trait. The next model to activate is an enemy Blood Servant, who attacks Carolina. Because of the Inspiration she receives +1D to her defense goal roll. When Radu activates on his turn he chooses to charge a second Blood Servant 8" away. Radu receives +1D to his attack goal roll from Inspiration. If the Blood Servant he attacks survives and attacks him back, he gets +1D on his defense goal roll, because it was his next available one after being inspired.

IRON WILL

The model's rating in Iron Will is added to its Resolve Goal rolls to resist certain other traits and to remain standing after reaching KO. Iron Will may not be used on Post-Battle tables.

KILLING STRIKE

This trait may be used a number of times indicated by the model's profile in the warband lists. Models using Killing Strike must announce their intent to do so before attacking a foe in close combat. If the attack succeeds, and forces its target to make a KO check, increase the TN of this check by +1.

Example: *A werewolf declares its using Killing Strike and hits in close combat. Its target fails to resist all of the damage and loses its last Vitality, forcing a KO check. The check would normally be TN3 for this attack, but because of Killing Strike it is now TN4.*

KNIFE-FIGHTER

Models possessing this trait are expert at killing with short, bladed weapons, mostly knives. A knife-fighter wounds foes more easily, and adds +1 DN to knives and throwing knives when he succeeds by 2+ goals instead of 3+. Additionally, the knife-fighter may never be disarmed when using knives or throwing knives.

LEADER

Models possessing this trait make natural leaders, capable of inspiring their bands and taking decisive action. In the dice-based initiative, levels in this trait add dice to the leader's initiative goal roll. In the card-based initiative, leaders are dealt extra cards equal to the trait's level during the initiative phase.

LIGHTNING REFLEXES

Models possessing this trait are dealt extra cards during the initiative phase. A model may only ever use one card for initiative, but this trait allows the model to choose which one it wants.

If using the dice-based initiative, models possessing lightning reflexes add +1 die to their designated leader's initiative goal roll dice per level of the trait.

MESMERIZE

This trait may be used a number of times indicated by the model's profile in the warband lists. Models possessing this trait may make up to an 8" gaze attack pitting their Mind against their target's Mind. Models with the Animal trait receive +2 dice to resist this attack. This attack counts as a special action.

If the attacker wins the target suffers -2" to its Move value on its next turn for each goal the attacker succeeds by, and grants foes +1 die to attack and defense goal rolls (total, regardless of goals succeeded by) until the pinning effect clears at the end of their next turn.

If the movement reduction gained by the attacker exceeds the target's normal movement allowance, the attacker can immediately move the target model the difference and conduct a combat action with the model. A Mesmerized model may not use charge movement! Note that the object of this attack does gain the +1 to its defense roll.

Example: *Mentar the mysterious attempts to Mesmerize Igor, a Manservant. Mentar scores five goals to the hapless Igor's one. Igor suffers -8" to his movement. Igor's normal movement allowance if 5", so Mentar may move Igor up to 3" and make an attack with him if possible.*

MIST FORM

A master vampire is a crafty and cunning foe, often slipping away at the last moment,

Special Traits

avoiding capture an ensuring he will return to plague the heroes at some later date. Vampires possessing this trait may be removed from play at the end of their turn anytime after the second round of the game. Models wishing to use this ability must be able to use a special action. Their player announces the trait's use, then removes the model. KO'ed models may not invoke this ability. Only one model per warband may possess this trait.

Vampires using this ability may not escape with any scenario objectives or other objects that were not on their profiles when the game began.

PACK MULE

Models possessing this trait are particularly adept at carrying large loads. Pack Mule models can carry up to Strength x 3 points of Encumbrance, rather than the normal Strength x 2. Additionally, models possessing Pack Mule may carry pieces of equipment for other models, handing them off using a special action.

RESOURCES

Models possessing this trait grant their warbands additional funds with which to purchase starting equipment and support further operations. Resources provide the warband with an additional 25 GBP at the start of a campaign and +5 GBP during each upkeep phase.

SCHOLAR

Models possessing this trait may add its dice to their Mind goal rolls when attempting to solve scenario objectives that require specialized knowledge (i.e., reading an ancient text, unlocking a puzzle or trap, etc.). Scholar models may also add their dice to Mind checks during the post-battle sequence to generate resources for their warbands.

SHAPE OF THE BAT

This trait may be used a number of times indicated by the model's profile in the warband lists. Vampires possessing this trait expend uses of it to transform into a bat form that allows them to fly above the battlefield, eluding the close combat attacks of their foes.

When a vampire expends a use of this trait its player should replace the vampire model with an appropriate bat model. The transformation lasts until the beginning of the model's next turn. While in bat form the vampire flies above the battlefield, out of reach of all close combat attacks.

This transformation does not allow the vampire to leave close combat without suffering free attacks as normal. However, the vampire (now in bat form) receives +1 die to its Agility to avoid these attacks.

Activating this trait counts as a charge that allows the vampire to cover extra distance. It may not attack while in this form. The bat-form may be placed above any piece of terrain on the board no matter the height.

While in bat form the vampire may carry scenario objectives or other ENC 1 (or less) items. At the beginning of its next turn the vampire model replaces the bat model. If the bat model was hovering above a rooftop or other high space, the vampire is placed in the space nearest where the bat was hovering.

SHAPE OF THE BEAST

This trait may be used a number of times indicated by the model's profile in the warband lists. Vampires possessing this trait expend uses of it to transform into a bestial form better suited to the rigors of close combat. Transforming counts as a free action and lasts until the beginning of the vampire's next turn.

While in its bestial shape the vampire model should be replaced with a more appropriate model to avoid confusion (werewolf, man-bat, and other hybrid models work well for this). A vampire's bestial form grants it +1 die to DR and Agility until the beginning of its next turn when it returns to normal.

If vampire possesses multiple uses of this power it may expend them on consecutive

Special Traits

turns to maintain its transformation. While in beast form the vampire may use any of his other special traits like Vampiric Might.

Example: *Vaclav the Nosferatu possesses two uses of Shape of the Beast. Beset by three monster hunters, he decides to transform*

Special Traits

into his man-bat form on his next turn. He activates his trait using a free action and his player removes the vampire model and replaces it with a man-bat model.

Vaclav enjoys +1 to Agility and DR until the beginning of his next turn. Surviving the human onslaught, Vaclav's next turn comes up and he expends his second use of Shape of the Beast to continue in his man-bat form. Vaclav will return to normal at the beginning of his next turn.

SHARP SENSES

Acute hearing, excellent night vision, hair-trigger neck hairs, or a keen sense of smell are all examples of Sharp Senses. Dice in this trait may be added to Mind goal rolls to spot objectives, hiding models, or anything else that might require a perception check.

SOLITARY

Solitary models prefer to work alone, and because of this, do not receive bonus dice from friends in close combat. However, friendly models in close combat with a solitary model still receive bonus dice from friends in close combat.

SPEED BURST

This trait may be used a number of times indicated by the model's profile in the warband lists. Speed Burst gives the model +3" of movement when activated. A model may use speed burst any time during of its turn.

TERRIFYING AURA

Some models are so alien and horrifying that approaching or even attacking them is difficult. At the beginning of its turn, any enemy model within 10" of a model possessing Terrifying Aura must make a TN3 Resolve (plus any Iron Will) goal roll or be Terrified. Models possessing Terrifying Aura receive +2 Dice on attack and defense goal rolls against models they have Terrified. Models using Held Actions make their check for this trait when they first activate and elect to go on hold.

Once a model has passed its Terrifying Aura check against a model, it does not need to make another one against that particular model for the remainder of the scenario.

Models possessing this trait ignore the effects of other Terrifying Auras.

TOUGH

Characters who are Tough sometimes prove harder to take down than normal. Tough characters enjoy 1 re-roll on DR checks, Resolve checks for KO, and Resolve checks for post-battle tables.

TRUE FAITH

Model's possessing this trait should also invest in a holy symbol of some sort. On his action, a holy man may try to use his True Faith to drive a vampire backward. This counts as a special action, and has an ER of 3".

The model wielding the ready holy symbol must win an opposed Resolve check with the vampire model. The holy model may add its Iron Will to this roll as well. If the holy man wins, the vampire is driven back (directly away) 2" for every goal the holy man wins by.

If the vampire wins, it holds its position, if it wins by 3 goals or more, the symbol bursts into flame, or becomes icy cold, and falls from the cleric's hand as if he had been disarmed.

This compulsory move is made immediately after the opposed rolls, and should the movement result in the vampire falling from a cliff, castle, or other high spot, falling damage is rolled normally. Vampires backed into corners, walls, or other impassable areas by this power are shaken and less capable in battle. Foes attacking a vampire in this state receive +1 die to ranged and close combat attacks until the end of the vampire's next turn.

True Faith models possessing a ready holy symbol also receive +1 die to attack and defense goal rolls against models with the Vampire special trait.

True Faith models may also bless the weapons of their comrades. This requires a special action and a TN3 Resolve goal roll. This may

Special Traits

be attempted once on each friendly model in the warband. If the roll succeeds, blessed weapons enjoy +1 DN against Vampire models. This blessing does not work on firearms, but does work on crossbows, stakes, and normal or silver close combat weapons.

Only one model per warband may possess this trait.

UNIQUE

A unique model is a one-of-a-kind character. There may never be more than one of a Unique model on a single warband. However, many impostors and pretenders populate the world of CIC, and it is possible to have the same Unique characters face-off as members of opposing warbands.

VAMPIRE

Models with this trait are vampires similar to the ones in the classic Bram Stoker novel, Dracula. Although many vampires also possess a host of other special traits that make them preternaturally strong and tough, their primary attribute is the ability to drain the very life from a victim by sucking his or her blood.

In order for a vampire to use his life-draining ability, he must successfully strike a foe in close combat, and instead of applying damage, he bites his prey. This bite occurs automatically, but in order to drain precious life essence from his target, the vampire must make a TN3 resolve goal roll.

If the roll succeeds the vampire drains 1 Vitality from the target model with no opposed damage resistance goal roll. A vampire that attacks in this manner regains one lost Vitality point, but can never gain more Vitality than its starting total.

Vampires at zero Vitality who drain a foe in this manner and move back up to positive Vitality must make a second KO check if they are subsequently dropped back to zero or lower.

If a Vampire drains a foe of her last Vitality point in this manner, and the foe fails his Resolve check to avoid KO, and is subsequently taken out of action by the vampire, the model

stands a chance of becoming a vampire as well! During the post-battle sequence, the victim must make a TN3 Resolve goal roll or she becomes a vampire. It is assumed that the victim's comrades sense her transformation and quickly put her out of her misery with a stake through the heart!

However, the player may wish to spare the model, in which case her comrades take pity and keep the character locked up. Although technically still part of the warband, the model may not be used for any scenarios unless a special circumstance dictates otherwise. If the vampire who slew the character is ever destroyed, any models it infected with its curse are freed.

Firearms are particularly ineffective against vampires. A vampire may re-roll up to three (3) failed damage resistance dice (i.e., dice rolling results of 1-3) when struck by a shot from a firearm.

Vampiric Weaknesses

Vampire models suffer from certain inherent weaknesses.

Wooden stakes through the heart can cripple or slay a vampire, and a model armed with a wooden stake may do just that. A model attacking a vampire with a wooden stake must make a successful close combat or ranged attack and succeed by 3 goals in order to place the stake in the vampire's heart. In addition to the normal damage, the vampire is immobilized. A vampire immobilized by a stake is vulnerable to total destruction. An immobilized vampire may be destroyed by any adjacent model that spends a combat action to finish them off by twisting the stake the final vital inches and destroying the creature's dark heart completely.

A friendly model may remove the stake from the vampire's heart only if there are no enemy models in base contact with it.

Holy Symbols wielded by a cleric, priest, or holy man possessing the True Faith trait can ward off a vampire. See the True Faith trait for more information on how this works.

Special Traits

Vampires suffer reduced DR versus Blessed Weapons (see the True Faith trait above).

Sunlight is the bane of all vampires; they cannot abide it. It is assumed that most scenarios involving a vampiric warband take place at night or in the darkness of a cave or cellar. If for whatever reason a vampire finds itself exposed to direct sunlight it loses all Vitality and must make an immediate KO check at the start of its turn. If this check is failed the Vampire is removed from play, and may be destroyed. If the check is passed the Vampire can do nothing save move toward the nearest area of shelter. Each turn it must make another KO check or face destruction.

VAMPIRIC MIGHT

This trait may be used a number of times indicated by the model's profile in the warband lists. Models using Vampiric Might must announce their intent to do so before attacking a foe in close combat. If the attack succeeds, they may add +1 to attack's DN#.

Vampires may also expend uses of this trait to burst through walls up to 2" thick. This counts as 2" worth of the model's Move value.

Vampire models may also expend use of this trait to make standing leaps of up to twice their Strength in inches. This leap may be vertical or horizontal, and may be preceded by a normal move up to 3". The total leap and movement counts as a charge, and if the model ends up in contact with an enemy, it may attack with the normal +2 dice for charging.

WALL-CRAWLER

Models possessing this trait treat vertical surfaces as if they were normal ground, and can charge up or down them as well. Players should mark a model's progress along a wall with a die or other method to let everyone exactly where they are.

WEREWOLF

Models with this trait are shape-shifters capable of taking the monstrous form of a half-wolf half-man. They possess amazing strength, speed, and recuperative powers.

Werewolves are extremely susceptible to weapons composed of silver, but most other weapons are particularly ineffective against them. A werewolf may re-roll up to three (3) failed damage resistance dice (i.e., dice rolling results of 1-3) when struck by blows from non-silver weapons. Fire is the only exception to this; flaming weapons like torches do normal damage to werewolves.

Werewolves are also powerful physical specimens capable of feats of superhuman strength. They receive +2D when making rolls to burst through doors.

They may also make standing vertical leaps of up to twice their Strength in inches. These leaps count as special actions and replace the normal jumping rules. Like animals, werewolves also receive +2D on normal jumping checks.

The Phases of the Moon

Unless playing a specific campaign scenario where the time and place are preset, a player running a werewolf pack should roll before each game to determine the current phase of the moon. A model with the Werewolf trait's power waxes and wanes as the moon does. The player rolls a D6:

1	New Moon (-1 all DN's)
2-5	Half Moon (traits normal)
6	Full Moon (+1 all DN's)

Werewolf Weaknesses

Werewolves suffer from a vulnerability to silver weapons. Silver weapons add +1 to their DN's versus werewolves, and werewolves struck by silver weapons do not get their normal DR re-rolls.

~6~

Equipment

VERY WEAPON AND ITEM comes under the general category of Equipment. Individual models can only carry a finite amount of Equipment without incurring a penalty to their Move value. A model possesses a carrying capacity equal to twice its Strength rating. This defines the amount of Encumbrance a model has to haul around its possessions.

A model can carry more, but for every point by which a model exceeds its carrying capacity, it suffers a -1" Move penalty per turn. Models may always choose to drop gear during the course of a game, but doing so may result in its loss.

Some items, weapons, or other equipment is so light as to have a minor effect on a model's movement. Items of this nature are marked with a "-/" in the ENC entry, and have no effect on a model's ENC total.

Players may not purchase large stores of items for their models and then choose to store them elsewhere. Even though every warband is thought to have a secure base of operations, game balance dictates that a piece of equipment bought for a model must be carried on the model's person.

By extension, players purchase equipment for individual models, not for the warband, so unless a model or henchmen group possesses the Pack Mule special trait, it is not permissible for it to carry equipment (especially weapons) for other models, and then pass them over when the model wants to use them. This circumvents the encumbrance rules and is generally bad form.

Equipment

Friendly or enemy models may pick up the equipment and weapons of KO'ed or Coup de Graced models using a special action. A warband that captures a model may also elect to keep or sell its equipment.

One special action allows the retrieval of one piece of equipment. If this results in an enemy model finishing a game with a purloined piece of equipment, then that enemy gets to keep that piece of equipment. Models with restrictions on the equipment they may use still must abide by these restrictions, and cannot use scavenged items in play, but still may take them and sell them later.

SELLING BACK ITEMS

Equipment (weapons and items) may be sold back at half its stated value. Players should round fractional values up or down normally.

Equipment scavenged from henchmen groups is of an inferior quality and counts as only twice the normal cost of the item for re-sale purposes.

Example: *A group of treasure hunters tries to sell back some swords it recovered from some slain Cossacks. A sword normally costs 6 GBP, and so the swords from the Henchmen group counts as one 12 GBP item which may be sold back for a profit of 6 GBP.*

ITEMS

Items can cover a wide range of equipment, from Rope to Armor to Medical Kits, and anything in between. Each Item listed below is purchased with points and carried by models in the Warband. Like weapons, some Items may cost Encumbrance.

FORBIDDEN LORE

Description: Forbidden Lore represents a character's research into obscure occult scrolls, tomes, and transcripts. A player must decide that his model is using Forbidden Lore before initiative is determined, and only one point may be used per round.

Depending on the initiative method agreed upon, a model using Forbidden Lore is either dealt one extra card for Initiative or allows his side's leader to add 1 the initiative roll, but begins its turn with -2" Move. Models using Forbidden Lore may not charge. Once a point of Forbidden Lore has been used it is gone for the rest of the game.
Cost: 1 pt per use
ENC: 1 per 2 GBP

GARLIC
Description: The cloves of this pungent root can sometimes ward off the undead. Sometimes. Fresh garlic must be purchased after each battle to remain effective. Models carrying garlic gain +1 die to defense goal rolls versus vampires with a weakness to it (see the post-battle section for more on Vampiric Weaknesses).
Cost: 1 GBP/battle
ENC: -/

HOLY SYMBOL
Description: A Crucifix, Star of David, or Crescent of Mohammed. The Holy Symbol allows a model possessing True Faith to channel his or her godly might against Vampires.
Cost: 2 GBP
ENC: -/

BULL'S EYE LANTERN
Description: A bull's eye lantern provides a party with light in a similar way to a torch, but with key differences. A bull's eye lantern provides more focused light. At the player's option, it negates any darkness conditions in only a 3" radius from the bearer, but can project a beam out to 15" in any one direction to illuminate one model or object. This counts as a special action for the bearer.

If the player desires, the model holding the lantern can cancel its radius effect to preserve the benefits of darkness for nearby comrades. This can de done as a free action, but must be clearly stated by the player.

Models or objects thus illuminated may be

Equipment

charged or targeted for ranged combat by any model, regardless of any darkness conditions. A lantern may also be thrown at an enemy model as an act of desperation. This counts as a normal combat action with a max range of 12".

Models successfully struck will catch fire on a 5+ and if alight will subsequently suffer a DN3 hit every round until extinguished via a special action as explained in the damage section. Obviously any lantern thrown will be useless and the party will need to purchase a new one after this battle if they wish to continue using one!
Cost: 4 GBP
Enc: 2

LUCKY CHARM

Description: A lucky rabbit's foot. The Roman coin from a past life. The bullet that didn't quite kill you. The old pocket bible that stopped a knife thrust. Lucky charms are talismans that some characters believe can keep them safe. Once per game, the model may re-roll any one dice pool throw, or force a foe to re-roll one throw that would have affected it.

The model chooses the better of the two throws for its circumstances. Henchmen groups may not have Lucky Charms, and only one model per warband may purchase a Lucky Charm. Other special traits that grant re-rolls may still be used on the second throw for a Lucky Charm.
Cost: 5 GBP
ENC: -/

MEDICAL BAG

Description: This item can come in a number of forms: a doctor's bag, a hedge wizard's pouch of herbs, or a charlatan's miracle cure-all. Models possessing levels in the Healer Trait can use a Medical Bag to help restore lost Vitality points to a model. Medical Kits add +2 dice to the Healer model's Mind goal roll when treating injured or KO'ed models.
Cost: 4 GBP
ENC: 1

PACK/WEAPON HARNESS

Cost: 2 GBP
Description: Piece of gear or clothing that aids in efficiently carrying weapons and equipment. May carry up to 2 pts. of Encumbrance.
ENC: -/

ROPE

Description: This 20" length of corded leather or woven fibers allows a model to climb vertical surfaces at its normal movement rate. A player must use a special action to set the rope on the climbing surface.
Cost: 2 GBP
ENC: 2

TORCH

Description: A torch provides illumination in darkness. Models carrying torches can mitigate darkness scenario conditions in a 6" radius around them. Models or objects thus illuminated may be charged or targeted for ranged combat by any model, regardless of any darkness conditions.

Torches may also be used as makeshift clubs. A torch has DN2 and if a model successfully strikes a foe with one, the target might catch fire. If a torch is used as a club, roll a die. On a 4+ it remains lit, otherwise it goes out. Re-lighting a torch requires a special action.
Cost: 2 GBP
ENC: 1

WOLF'S BANE

Description: A poisonous European herb of yellowish color that is extremely dangerous to werewolves. Models possessing wolf's bane who battle werewolves in close combat receive +1 die to defense goal rolls against them. Fresh wolf's bane must be purchased after each battle.

Up to two models in a campaign may begin the first game with Wolf's Bane, but acquiring it after the first battle is difficult. Wolf's Bane counts as a Rare Item, and must be searched for as detailed in post-battle rules in Chapter VII. One model may search for the entire warband, and if he succeeds, he finds enough

for everyone for the next battle. It still must be paid for as normal.

Cost: 1 GBP/battle

ENC: -/

WEAPONS

Weapons are special kinds of Equipment that often have special abilities, and these are described in the section following the weapon listings. As explained in the combat section in Part II, a weapon's damage number (DN) is the target number foes must match or beat to avoid suffering Vitality loss.

Models possessing Strength 4 or greater add +1 to the DN's of the close combat weapons that they wield.

CLOSE COMBAT WEAPONS

BATTLEAXE

Description: Shaft of wood mounting heavy, single-edged, wedge-shaped blade.

Cost: 5

DN: 6

Special: -1D close combat attack

ENC: 2

CLUB/TRUNCHEON

Description: Bludgeoning weapon composed of solid wood, sometimes tipped with metal banding or wrapped in a leather thong.

Cost: 3

DN: 3

Special: none

ENC: 1

KNIFE/SHORT SWORD

Description: Shorter than a sword or saber, a short sword or knife is ideal for fighting in enclosed areas.

Cost: 4

DN: 4

Special: none

ENC: 1

MAKESHIFT CLUB

Description: Walking staff, rifle butt, large stone, etc.

Cost: n/a

DN: 3

Special: -1D CC Defense

ENC: 1

SPEAR

Description: A pole arm with a single blade on one end, employed with sweeping, or thrusting motion. May also be thrown.

Cost: 5 pts.

DN: 4

ER: 5"

Special: +1D CC Defense against charging foes, Extra Reach 1"

ENC: 2

SWORD/SABER

Description: Swords come in many varieties, but this category of weapon describes any edged blade between 2 1/2 and 3 ft. in length.

Cost: 8

DN: 5

Special: +1D CC Defense

ENC: 1

THROWING KNIFE

Description: This describes any small, aerodynamic blade that can be wielded in close combat, but is more likely thrown at range. A model is assumed to possess enough knives to last it the entire battle.

Cost: 4

DN: 3

ER: 3"

Special: Enemies armed with larger ENC weapons receive +1D CCD against foes using a weapon of this type against them in Close Combat.

ENC: -/

WOODEN STAKE

Description: These sharpened shafts of wood are especially useful for taking out pesky vampires.

Cost: 2 GBP (brace of three stakes)

DN: 3

Special: On successful strikes that beat the

Equipment

vampire's defense by 4+ goals, the attack may hit the heart adding +4 to the DN.
ENC: 1

RANGED WEAPONS

CROSSBOW

Description: Ranged weapon consisting of a bow fixed across a wooden stock, having a groove or barrel for the missile and a mechanism for holding and releasing the string.
Cost: 10
DN: 5
ER: 12"
Special: Slow
ENC: 2

HOLY WATER

Description: Water blessed by the power of God becomes a deadly weapon against models with the Vampire special trait. Holy Water must be re-purchased after every battle in which it is used.
Cost: 4
DN: 6
ER: 3"
Special: Only works against Vampires; Radius 2"; may also be used in close combat with a standard opposed roll; extra goals in close or ranged combat do not increase DN, but vampires do not get their normal re-rolls to DR as with other ranged attacks.
ENC: -/

PISTOL (ARCHAIC)

Description: Any of a number of single-handed firearms using matchlock or flintlock technology.
Cost: 7
DN: 4
Special: Slow
ER: 8"
ENC: 2

PISTOL/REVOLVER (LIGHT)

Description: Any number of small caliber firearms including .22 revolver, .38 special, or Mauser auto-pistol.
Cost: 8

DN: 4
ER: 8"
Special: none
ENC: 1

PISTOL/REVOLVER (HEAVY)

Description: Any number of large caliber firearms including .44 revolver, .45 pistol, etc.
Cost: 10
DN: 5
ER: 10"
Special: none
ENC: 1

RIFLE (ARCHAIC)

Description: Any of a number of longer-range firearms using matchlock or flintlock technology.
Cost: 11
DN: 5
Special: Slow
ER: 12"
ENC: 2

RIFLE (MODERN)

Description: Any of a number of longer-range firearms usually loaded by means of a bolt or lever-action chamber.
Cost: 16
DN: 6
Special: none
ER: 15"
ENC: 2

SAWED-OFF SHOTGUN

Description: Pistol firing a spread of small, metallic pellets.
Cost: 7
DN: 4
ER: 5"
Special: Radius 2"
ENC: 1

SHOTGUN

Description: Long-barreled smoothbore weapon firing a spread of small, metallic pellets.
Cost: 10
DN: 4
ER: 10"
Special: Radius 1"
ENC: 2

AMMUNITION

Chaos in Carpathia is a heroic miniature combat game, and in keeping with that tone, players shouldn't worry about keeping track of their ammunition unless a scenario special event or special weapon trait dictates otherwise. Players should assume that a model carries enough ammunition to see it through the entire battle.

OPTIONAL RULE-AMMO/JAM CHECKS

Players can add extra detail (and drama) to ranged combat with this rule. Whenever a model scores 0 goals on a ranged attack goal roll, its weapon has become jammed, run out of ammo, or suffered some other difficulty. In order to fire it again, the model must use a special action to clear the jam, reload, or re-string the weapon.

WEAPON SPECIAL CHARACTERISTICS

DEFENSE BONUS

Effects: Some weapons make it easier for a model to defend itself in Close Combat, or make it easier for foes to defend against them under certain circumstances. These weapons are noted in the descriptions above as +1D CC Defense, and models defending with them receive +1D to defense Agility goal rolls.

DEFENSE PENALTY

Effects: Some weapons make it harder for a model to defend itself in Close Combat. These weapons are noted in the descriptions above as -1D CC Defense, and models defending with them receive -1D to defense Agility goal rolls.

EXTRA REACH

Effects: Rated in inches, Extra Reach allows a character to make close combat attacks outside of base contact. Models under attack from a foe possessing a weapon with Extra Reach are considered to be in close combat for purposes of determining multiple foe bonuses and leaving combat.

RADIUS

Effects: Weapons with this feature add an area effect to the attack that has a variable radius (rated in inches) from the base of the primary target. All models touched by the radius of the attack must make a defense goal roll against the attacker's goal roll. Weapons with Radius will be noted in their descriptions in this manner: Radius (X"), where X is the number of inches of the effect.

SILVER (RARE ITEM)

Effects: For +2 GBP any close combat weapon may be composed of silver. Firearms with this trait are loaded with silver-tipped bullets, and cost +5 GBP. Silver weapons add +1 DN against models with the Werewolf trait. Silver weapons are rare and only 2 models per warband may begin the campaign with them, and each of the two models may only be armed with one type. Henchmen may never possess silver weapons.

As rare items, additional silver weapons and ammunition may be sought out in the post-battle phase by a warband. If they are found, they will allow the warband to exceed the starting allotment of two silver weapons. The particulars of this process are detailed in Chapter VII: Campaigns.

Example: *Aaron is running a band of monster hunters. He buys a silver sword for one of his models and silver bullets for another. He has now reached his allowance of silver-armed models. It is assumed after each battle that these models care for their weapons and see that they are ready for the next encounter.*

SLOW

Effects: Models may only move half their normal Move and still fire in the same turn. Models using slow weapons who also wish to use the Aim maneuver may not move at all on the turn they fire their weapon.

~7~

Campaigns

CAPTAIN JACK PAGE HAD ONCE VOWED to restore the fortunes of his family and the oath had presently taken him to the Southern Carpathians, deep in the Adanca valley at the foot of the jagged Moralului ridges. It was a long way from home. He and his clan were destitute since Sherman had put a torch to the family's estates and his current situation would brook no hesitation when it came to opportunity. The women of the Page family and those young enough to have escaped duty in Lee's army eked out a precarious existence back home while Jack sought out work.

Though regarded as a task beneath the dignity of such a gentleman as himself, his current errand made excellent use of his many talents. A prepossessing figure blessed with classical good looks, the broad shouldered captain could draw from a deep well of physical courage and an indomitable hardiness that saw him through the worst of the North's war of aggression. His somewhat average intelligence was favorably augmented by a good education and a sort of animal cunning known to run in the men of the Page family.

All these assets were well exercised by his current business, satisfying the lust for objects of antiquity known to nest in the hearts of academics and the idle rich.

It was a strange game, well suited to Page's dogged determination and ability to inspire loyalty among his fellow travelers. One was ill advised to travel alone in some of the places Captain Page was known to venture. While the roster of fellow adventurers around him might change from errand to errand, Page's

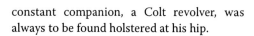

Campaigns

constant companion, a Colt revolver, was always to be found holstered at his hip.

"Captain Page, according to the Frenchman's map we should be getting close. Perhaps only a day or two more." said Matei, a Rumanian that came highly recommended by some of Page's associates in London. His language skills had been indispensable.

Page glanced at the map and then around in frustration at the many pines that pressed in against the trail, obscuring any attempt to find a landmark. Their fragrant scent was carried on the chill air, heavy with damp from the autumn rains. The exertions had warmed the party so where most had taken off their coats, all except Dubois, the Frenchman who had contracted the services of Jack and his band. He shuffled along, bundled in layer after layer of tweed, still complaining of chill. The captain had unbuttoned his worn cavalryman's jacket to the waist. A sweat dampened shirt of coarse cream linen clung to his broad chest. His sandy brown curls were held swept back with an oil that smelled lightly of cinnamon.

Jack led the column with Matei close behind. The Frenchman ambled along in the middle followed by David MacDonald, a buffalo hunter from Dakota, and Aga, a massive Turk from the Anatolian steppe. Aga led the group's pack mule.

MacDonald and Aga were comfortable in the outdoors. Both were reputed to be serious men, nonplussed by physical danger. MacDonald kept a close tongue in his head while Aga rambled on in his broken English that he had learned during a stint on a merchant vessel. Aga's sport had become the challenge of eliciting laughter from the taciturn MacDonald.

The party gathered along the wide trail as Matei pocketed the map and Jack considered his options. Aga stood with arms folded above his twin pistols while Macdonald peered at Jack from under a tattered hat, the band strung with small bones. He balanced his massive rifle atop his shoulders, arms hung over either

ends. Dusk was an hour away and the map promised a village some miles ahead. The prospect of a proper meal factored heavily in the captain's mind.

"We'll pick up the pace a bit and then bed down in the village. Hopefully there will be some accommodation. I don't fancy sleeping in the rain again. Dubois, I'm afraid your Dacian gold will have to wait yet another day."

Dubois shrugged, imitating the stoicism of his rough companions, "It has waited a millennium, a day or two more should not concern it.

Two hours later the sun had dipped below the mountains, bathing the jagged horizon in an azure glow. The party trudged onward, the dark amidst the ancient trail deepening every moment. Jack peered down the trail, squinting into the gloom. His irritation was evident in the timber of his fine Georgian accent.

"Matei, where is this village? I believe we should have reached it by now."

Matei shrugged, his arms raised, "Captain, I am from Bucharest."
A sharp look from Page silenced further comment. His hand massaged the short, blond beard on his chin as he pondered the party's options. Finding a clearing off the trail and setting up camp seemed the only course left open. He scanned the wood line. The forest was growing quiet. A changing of the guard was taking place.

Diurnal creatures were bedding down for the evening as the nocturnal were stirring, emerging from lairs of pine needles and moist earth to begin another night of hunting or foraging. Eyes attuned to darkness waited with the patience of an ancient earth as the last rays of the sun melted beneath the horizon. Jack issued orders, his voice suddenly overloud in the intimate gloom of new night.

"MacDonald, see if there is somewhere to camp to the left. I'll go right. Aga, break out the torches." The grizzled hunter obeyed

Campaigns

wordlessly while Aga hummed a tune as he worked, unpacking a strongbox from the party's docile mule. Dubois stood aloof. MacDonald returned in moments, calling Page back to the trail. In his gravelly voice, never much above a whisper, he informed Jack of a clearing not far at all from the trail, a patch of grass at the base of a rocky hill. Macdonald gestured curtly for Page to follow.

Dubois held the torch while Aga attempted to light the match, hampered by his sausage fingers, knobby and bent from the violent

Campaigns

work with which he was apt to employ them.

"Monsieur, allow me."

Dubois took the matches and handed him the torch, now working by touch as the dark worsened. With his gloves of fine leather the scholar nimbly dragged the match against the abrasive surface of the box. A crackling hiss and the match burst into orange flame. Dubois could see clearly Aga's scarred face suddenly awash in the glow, and behind him, another face where there should have been none. Dubois screamed and dropped the match, blackness flooded back in like water from a burst dam.

Aga spun, dropping the torch and drawing his pistols. He could make out nothing beyond vague shapes around the orange blob seared for the moment onto his retinas. He spat a curse in his native Turkish.

"What is it?"

"Mon dieu, I saw a woman behind you. She fled into the woods, off to the right, I think." Macdonald and Page sprinted back from the clearing just off the trail. Aga explained before Jack had begun to ask.

"Dubois was scared by a girl he says he saw. She must have been a peasant walking the trail."

"Gods below, Dubois, I thought you'd been attacked by wild beasts."
Aga began to chuckle, a rumbling sound from deep in his belly while Macdonald's lined faced cracked into a wry grin. Matei laughed as he picked up the dropped torch.

"All well and good amis, but it gave me quite a start."

A sound from the woods tore through the group's low laughter, a sound that reached back through the gray mists of time into prehistory. It was the howl of a wolf. The sound rang out amidst the pine trees and rocky hills, an echoing, plaintive wail tinged with a desperate hunger. The party was a

disparate group of individuals from a variety of backgrounds spread across multiple continents. But all knew, from vertiginous wells of a common ancestral memory, that the forest was no longer exclusively theirs. Another predator, older and more savage, was in the forest tonight.

Jack's throat tightened and his mouth was suddenly dry. Macdonald was the first to move. With swift and silent motions he began to unpack extra ammunition from one of the bundles on the mule's back. His face, now cloaked in near complete darkness, turned to Jack. His gravelly whisper broke the pregnant silence. He spoke one word.

"Close."

The captain shrugged off the passing fear. He knew wolves wouldn't attack a group of men unless they were desperately hungry or had been given no option to flee. The group of men was five strong and armed. There was nothing to cause concern.

From further away a chorus of howls answered the first. Icy needles ran down the length of Matei's spine. The mule brayed and begun to pull at its reins. Aga pulled the reins taut and patted the creature's head, calming it. MacDonald had loaded his rifle with a smoothness and silence born from thousands of repetitions and now crouching low, he began to creep toward the trail's edge, a border that separated man's domain and the wolf's. He whispered over his shoulder to Jack.

"He's on top of that hill. Maybe 'hundred yards. That call was to let his friends know we're here. Must've been stalking that girl."

Dubois was an urbane sort of man, most at home in the drawing room enjoying the thrust and parry of stimulating conversation. The wolves' primeval songs had left no impression on him beyond the initial start. His voice rang out in the crisp dark.

"Well, enough of that. Startled twice in as many minutes! My heart will fail if this

Campaigns

continues like this. Monsieur MacDonald, are you leaving us to hunt this sad dog, howling in his woods?"

MacDonald smiled his grim smile, pausing to spit a globule of tobacco juice onto the trail.

"I don't think you understand, Frenchie. That "sad dog" was likely stalking that young girl you just met. We ruined his hunt and now's he's let his friends know we're here. Soon they'll all be here and the king will have to figure out what's next and all."

Dubois stood speechless. It was the most he had ever heard MacDonald speak during the whole of their journey. Apparently, while in his milieu, the man could be almost chatty. His surprise evaporating, Dubois found a question on his thin lips.

"The king, monsieur?"

"Every wolf pack has one. A king and a queen. They choose what the rest do. They'll come with the rest and look us over."

"And what then?"

"Probably nothing. They'll know better, smelling our weapons and all. It won't hurt to shoot one or two to make sure they know what's best."

Jack's classical features were bathed in the orange glow of the torch Aga had finally managed to light. His expression was awash with sudden concern.

"Wait a minute, MacDonald. We need to be worried about that girl. Poor thing tore off into the woods. What if the wolves are still after her? We should find her before they do."

MacDonald had rested his rifle's barrel on the low limb of a dead and bare pine standing skeletally just off the trail. Cheek resting on the weapon, he squinted into the gloom, mapping the brightening shapes of rocks and trees in the growing moonlight.

His voice was a mere mumble as he whispered while hunched over.

"The howls didn't say nothing about a girl."

Jack's aquiline brow creased in irritation. Time was slipping away while that girl ran through the darkness. Deep inside the captain a foreboding grew, like the ever loudening low whistle of a train approaching a platform in the dark. Instinct let its wishes be known in gestures beyond language, a twitch in his muscles, a certain taste in the mouth. All these spoke to Jack, telling him to stay on the trail. But his education, his long apprenticeship in the ways and obligations of a gentleman, these forced him to do otherwise. A young woman was in peril, running through the primeval murk, and there was only one option for Captain Page.

"Dubois said the girl fled to the right. A couple of wolves are no match for my pistol. MacDonald, come with me if you like, if not, don't shoot me as I return."

Wordlessly the grizzled hunter brought his rifle from the branch and moved to follow the captain. Aga spat at the ground, startling Dubois.

"No one will say Aga is coward!" The massive man lit another two torches, handing one to Jack and keeping one for himself as the three left the trail.

Matei and Dubois were left with the mule. Dubois threw up his hands in a characteristically French gesture conveying a complex array of sentiments ranging from mild surprise to a good natured fatalism. He turned to the tightly packed bundles resting on the mule's back.

"Now, where is my tobacco?"

The captain moved as fast as he could trust his footing on a forest floor wound with twisted roots and broken branches. MacDonald followed noiselessly while Aga swore at every twig that hindered his stride, crashing

Campaigns

through the brush in a flurry of meaty limbs punctuated with blasts of Turkish profanity. Page stopped in his tracks, a fragment of stark white had caught his eye.

MacDonald slid beside him and Aga halted, panting with the exertion. There hanging on a tree branch in the middle of the forest was a piece of clothing, a peasant's shirt Jack learned as he brought it down to inspect. Cuffs and a boat collar were embroidered with red and yellow threads. It was inside out, as if pulled off in a hurry.

The sound of a twig snapping underfoot was heard just behind the trio. All three reacted at once, spinning around and leveling weapons at a threat as yet unseen. From behind, again, came a sound of motion across the cluttered forest floor. This time it was unmistakable. The three were turned again, sighting down rifle and pistol barrels into the Stygian dark beyond the feeble torch light. As the three men stared they knew without a doubt, that somewhere in the blackness, eyes were staring back. Jack spat in disgust.

"Enough of this!" He walked with an authority and purpose, arrogantly into the blackness where he thought he had glimpsed the eerie glow of a beast's tapetum, the reflective layer at the back of the eyes. With sure footsteps Page was plunged ever deeper into a realm his species had left to others long ago, a realm of hunting and night, of a panting pursuit and raw meat black under moonlight.

The arc of torchlight preceded him, flowing over the ground, crawling up tree trunks, a guttering orange glow. Blocks of gray stone were revealed in the weak light, rough rectangles half submerged and laying at oblique angles to the ground. Whether shaped by nature's inexorable forces or crude human hands Jack could not tell.

He paused for a moment to examine one, as high as a man but of greater width. By chance the stone pointed toward the pale face of the full moon. The luminous gray disk was still low in the sky, just barely visible above

the trees that pressed in at every turn. He resumed his plodding forward. The edge of the torch illuminated a new shape, the outline of a human. Jack jogged forward, elated to have found the girl. He called back in his booming baritone, "I found her!"

The figure ahead seemed to coalesce from the blackness. It was not a woman, nor even a man. It stood as tall as the captain but hunched over, back heaving as it panted. Through a row of pointed carnivore's teeth its breath fogged in the chill air. Above the muzzle two eyes burned, red embers reflected in the torchlight.

It wore no clothes. The beast's muscular body was covered with a pelt of brown fur ticked with black. Though it stood on two legs there was no mistaking its nature. It was a beast, a thing of night and whispered folklore, a creature spawned outside the purview of the god to whom Jack was known to pray. The captain was no stranger to peril; he had met death on many occasions. Sometimes fortune had been his ally, a bullet striking where he had stood a moment before.

And sometimes he had forced fortune's hand with his indomitable will, dodging death with the spinning grace of a matador. None of his experiences had prepared him for this. Before him was a nightmare translated in flesh, a thing of unknowable origin even as its nature was plain. Growling, the wolf-thing raised a clawed hand to strike. Jack began to raise his pistol to fire, knowing even as he did that the beast's strike would hit before the weapon could save him. The captain's eyes stared deeply into the eyes of the beast, reflecting fully the light of the full moon.

The boom from MacDonald's rifle reverberated around the forest, a shock wave passing through the night. The beast flew back, howling in pain, as Jack was peppered with fragments of bone from the creature's shattered sternum. Tufts of fur floated down to the bed of pine needles. The thing lay motionless at Jack's feet. The curtain of primordial terror over his mind had been

Campaigns

rent at the sound of the gunshot, man's tools dispelling the dark. He found he could speak.

"Gods below..."

MacDonald whistled, calling Jack's attention back to the pair. MacDonald still wore his grim expression, unchanged. Aga looked blanched, even in the warm light of the torch. The hunter spat a mouthful of tobacco juice onto the forest floor.

"Best be stepping back, Captain."

Jack left the inert form of the beast behind as he jogged back to his companions. Aga mumbled a question.

"What...was..."

MacDonald squinted into the gloom, answering as he peered into the black depths.

"Skinwalker. Never seen one so close."

The forest around them stirred with sudden life. The three wordlessly shifted, standing back to back, weapons raised. Every shadow lurking at the edge of the torches' light was loaded with primal menace. The men became aware that they were being circled. The beast had not been alone and now his companions lurked at the light's edge, testing, smelling for weakness in their cornered prey.

"I tracked one once, going north up the Idaho panhandle. The thing had killed an injun boy and me and some of them tracked it. We made camp one night. I went on ahead, figuring it was following a stream and I wouldn't need the light to see its sign. I came back to the camp and they was all dead. Ripped apart. I got its trail back but then the snows came and I had to go back. It was just one."

"Looks like this is a bigger party, no?" Aga snickered, mustering his bravado so that he would face death like a man.

MacDonald answered, "Yea, but this is an older place, older than the oldest mountain in America."

The circling beasts began a chorus of growls and barks. The sounds were much deeper than a wolf's. Amidst the sounds Jack thought he could hear a sound stranger still, the low weeping of a woman. Jack squinted, desperate to penetrate the blackness and glimpse the source of the sound.

From the light's edge a figure emerged, a woman. She came in view ahead of MacDonald; Jack could see her over his left shoulder, the supple whiteness of her figure catching his eye. She was naked but walked without shame, her delicate feet stepping across the forest floor with an animal grace. Thin brows were arched in a fierce expression over a beautiful face partly covered by the locks of curly black hair that hung around her shoulders. Her eyes glowered as she approached, cheeks flushed and full lips pursed, hips swaying with her supple stride. The moonlight shined on her shoulders and breasts, glistening with sweat as her body gave off tendrils of steam that snaked sensual arcs in the chill air.

There was a petulant air about her, something in the angle of her head and her posture, one arm held behind her back. Jack was spellbound. Impulses competed in his mind, inaction reigned. MacDonald's grim mask had melted into an expression of shock. He stood paralyzed while Aga was simply unaware, attention focused to his front. The moonlit figure, a sudden goddess, presently stood before MacDonald. Her scarlet lips parted and she spoke, a pleasant voice twisted in anger.

Campaigns

"You shot my mate!" she screamed in Romanian, and though MacDonald could not understand her, the hatred in her voice was clear.

MacDonald and the captain stood uncomprehending while Aga wheeled around to see her. Her left arm came around from behind her back. Jack thought for a second that she wore some sort of elaborate glove but then realized with rising terror that the fur and the claws were all too real, real enough to open MacDonald's throat with her strike. The hunter's jugular sprayed gouts of blood onto the woman, covering her chest and abdomen with thick streaks of red black that steamed in the moon's cold light. She roared a sound impossible for a human, a sound of primordial exultation.

Jack's own call of fury joined the chorus as he fired, round after round into her chest. She reeled back, catching her balance as the weapon's hammer struck an empty chamber. But there was still shooting, Aga blasted away at targets Jack couldn't see. He could hear them though, a nightmare cacophony of growls and yelps. The woman dashed back to the forest's edge, seemingly no worse for her wounds.

Aga yelled, "I can barely hurt them! I shoot, they just move back!"

Shock after shock had numbed Jack's sense of reality and now he found he could act freely again, unrestrained by the need to make sense of his surroundings, an actor in a lucid dream.

"Grab MacDonald's rifle! It put one of the beasts down before."

Aga bent down to pick up the weapon and one of the wolf-things was on top of him in one quick breath. Claws raked his side and he swore, swinging upward with the rifle to land a mighty blow on the lupine head. The expression of hateful lust written on the animal face evaporated as the creature flew back, landing with a thud. Aga got the rifle nestled in his shoulder and now pointed it here and there, jerking back and forth as he strove to find a target. His torch sputtered on the ground, dying and leaving the pair with Jack's torch as the only source of light save the moon. The beasts held back, fearing the rifle. A stalemate had emerged.

Aga asked the captain calmly, his husky bass voice betraying only frustration, "Captain, do you have a plan?"
Jack eyes darted from shadow to shadow. The empty pistol was heavy in his hand; he could not hold the torch and load it. The clammy sweat of primal fear was on his back like the caress of dead hands. The muscles of his square jaw flexed as his core being rose to the fore. He was Captain Jack Page, gentleman and officer, an identity that would not let itself be lost in a furious storm of unexpected and dire events. He dropped the pistol and then without looking, reached back behind him to find Aga's second pistol and draw it from its holster on the big Turk's waist. Armed again, his mind raced in search of a course of action.

"A minute, Aga, I'll figure something out."

THE STORY SO FAR...

In the early days of his rule, Dracul, father of Dracula, prince of Wallachia, and founding member of the Order of the Dragon, ran afoul of a festering evil in the heart of Transylvania. Previous rulers in the region had made dark pacts with the Nameless Gods to achieve their political and personal ends. However, these pacts rarely worked out well for the mortals who made them. Both Ladislaus and Andreas fell to the seductive power of the minions of the Nameless Gods. Later in the 15th century, Dracul was visited by another member of the von Draken family, as it had by that time become fated that the family von Draken was to forever serve the cosmic and unknowable ends of the Nameless.

Arnim von Draken visited Dracul and plied him with his silver tongue and promises of immortality. But the Wallachian prince's honor and pride were too great, and he resisted, casting this latest von Draken from his court, and warning him never to return.

Campaigns

But Dracul's rule did not last forever, and when his son Dracula came to power, Arnim von Draken returned. The cruel and remorseless Vlad Dracula did not possess his father's honor or sense of duty to innocents. Half a lifetime of captivity living among the Turks had hardened him, and given him an implacable will that did not allow for the luxury of mercy. He was just the sort of ruler the Nameless were looking for.

Arnim von Draken initiated Dracula into the mysteries of his Nameless gods, and Dracula embraced these rites with wanton abandon. He bathed himself in the blood of innocents, and the Nameless rewarded him with immortality, and an undying thirst for blood. He developed other powers as well, along with ability to pass his curse along to select numbers of his victims.

But the gifts of the Nameless prove fickle at times, and Dracula's newfound might carried with it a curse. He could no longer abide the light of day, the sun's rays a withering force that could burn him and his undead kin as easily as any flame. It was this curse that forced the maddened Dracula from power, for as he slept by day he became easier prey for his many enemies.

SCENARIOS

Chaos in Carpathia provides players the opportunity to tell tales on the table-top. Each player runs a warband of monsters, monster hunters, or mercenaries in a Victorian era setting tinged with elements of the supernatural, the strange, and the chaotic.

Players tell these tales by playing linked games called scenarios. A number of scenarios strung together form a campaign. In campaign games, everything is amplified. Models take on real character and personality. They survive the travails of deadly combat, discover weird

artifacts, subjugate sleepy Romanian villages, or free terrified towns from monstrous tyranny. Along the way models may perish, or grow to become even greater heroes or villains.

Scenarios are made up of the following components:

NAME (The name of the scenario)

DESCRIPTION (the nature of the scenario)

SETUP (Where the models begin the scenario on the board)

SPECIAL RULES (Any special circumstances in the scenario)

OBJECTIVE (what each player must do to win the scenario)

END GAME (The number of rounds the game lasts and any special victory conditions which might exist in the scenario)

SCENARIO REWARDS (Details the additional experience models earn for participating in the scenario.)

SPECIAL EVENTS BOX (Contains a matrix of 1 - 3 complications players may choose at random to add extra interest to the battle. The specific details of each Special Event are detailed in a later section. Unless noted, players always roll for Special events prior to the setup of teams on the table.)

RANDOM SCENARIO SELECTOR (ROLL 1D6)
1. Terror in a Tiny Town
2. Meeting at Castle Dracula
3. Battle in the Wilderness
4. The Rescue
5. The Manor House
6. The Crypt

Campaigns

BATTLE IN THE WILDERNESS!

DESCRIPTION: The warbands meet amid the quiet seclusion of dense wilderness. Their meeting could be mere chance, or the culmination of a mutual hunt for one another. Alternately, perhaps some bit of sacred or profane ground is the prize in the battle.

SETUP: This scenario is fought in a heavily wooded or mountainous region of old Europe. The 4' x 4' board should be covered with several copses of trees or large rock formations, a stream, and plenty of scrub or other cover.

Players should then randomly select which side of the board their warbands will enter on. Players may then take turns placing their models up to 8" in on from their respective board edges. If they are close enough, models may be placed behind appropriate terrain.

SPECIAL RULES: Thick Woods! The thick wilderness this battle takes place in hampers movement and limits ranged attacks. All models suffer -1" to their normal Move value and only receive +3" on a charge.

Campaigns

Additionally, ranged attacks beyond 10" automatically miss their targets.

OBJECTIVE: Players battle until all opposition has been KO'ed, or until one player concedes defeat and flees the board.

END GAME: The game ends when one player has conceded, or all of an opposing Warband's opposition has been KO'ed.

SCENARIO REWARDS: +1 experience to winning warband members

SPECIAL EVENTS BOX	
1-2	Grudge Match
3-4	Fallen Temple
5-6	Stygian Darkness

TERROR IN A TINY TOWN

DESCRIPTION: This battle depicts the struggle for control of a small eastern European town. Why are the warbands fighting for control of the town? Perhaps the town contains a small church vital to the greater battle, or maybe one of the town's residents holds important knowledge about pending supernatural events. No matter the reason, it is vital that one warband control the town for at least that evening, so combat must ensue.

SETUP: Players should fight the scenario amid the cobblestone streets of an Eastern European town. Each player should take turns placing a building or other urban feature on the board until a 4' x 4' area is filled with terrain. At least six buildings or other features should be placed.

Players should then randomly select which side of the board their warbands will enter on. Players may then take turns placing their models up to 8" in on from their respective board edges. If they are close enough, models may be placed behind appropriate terrain, or inside buildings.

SPECIAL RULES: The Mob! The people of Danova do not take kindly to having their nights interrupted with wanton violence. Overcoming their fear, some of them have formed a mob to attack the interlopers and drive them from their village. The mob is a large henchmen group with the stats listed below.

At the beginning of the game each player chooses a member of the warband to make a Resolve goal roll. The warband with the higher total starts the game with control of the mob.

If a monstrous warband controls the mob, they've intimidated or ensorcelled them into doing their bidding. If monster or treasure hunters control the mob they have convinced them to aid them in battling the supernatural creatures that menace their town.

Either way, the mob starts the game as part of one of the warbands. The mob is dealt a card as normal in the card-based initiative, or nominated to act by the controlling player as a member of his warband in the dice-based initiative.

MOB

Str	Agl	Mnd	Res	Move	DR Pool	Fate	Vitality
2	2	2	3	5"	3	3	Henchmen (10 members)

Special Traits
Combat Attack x 1
Sharp Senses x 1

Equipment
Mob Weapons (Clubs and Kitchen Implements DN3)
Torches (DN2)

Campaigns

Wresting Control

During his turn, any model within 6" of the mob may use a special action to wrest control of the mob from the opposing warband. The model may make a Mind + Scholar goal roll to reason with the crowd and argue that they should join the opposing cause. Alternately, the model may make a Resolve + Iron Will check to try to intimidate the mob into changing sides. Both types of rolls are TN4 actions.

If the mob does switch sides, they do so on their next available turn.

OBJECTIVE: Drive the opposing warband from the town and pacify or kill the maddened townspeople.

END GAME: The game ends when one player has conceded, or all of an opposing Warband's opposition has been KO'ed.

SCENARIO REWARDS: +1 experience to winning warband members; +5 GBP to the winning warband.

SPECIAL EVENTS BOX	
1-2	Grudge Match
3-4	Coming of the Dawn
5-6	Stygian Darkness

MEETING AT CASTLE DRACULA

DESCRIPTION: This battle occurs atop the ruins and battlements of Castle Dracula, but could be fought in any castle or fortress location. The warbands involved have found themselves searching the highland country and both come upon a deserted castle that could contain hidden treasure or other resources.

SETUP: The battle takes place on a roughly 3' x 3' board that should comprise the ruins of a castle or keep. Ideally, the walls should feature battlements capable of supporting a skirmish involving multiple miniatures. The castle walls should include two break-points, or areas where the walls have crumbled to allow access from the ground. Also, a front gate with an open portcullis will create a third point of entry. Each point of entry should be roughly 12" or more from each other entry point.

Each player chooses a model to make a Mind + Sharp Senses goal roll. The model that scores more goals scouts the sight and chooses the best point of entry for his warband. Settle ties by re-rolling the contest until a winner emerges. The winning warband is then deployed within 8" of the entry point of its choice, but not inside the castle walls.

The losing warband must pick one of the remaining entry points, and deploys in the same manner as the winning band.

SPECIAL RULES: Searching the battlements, models may find clues or relics that either earn them extra experience or gain them extra income. Any model that finds itself atop the battlements may use a special action and make a TN4 Mind + Scholar or Mind + Sharp Senses goal roll.

A successful roll grants the model a rare find. Perhaps a piece of old parchment containing some ritual or historical note, or an old coin that holds extra value for collectors. If the model survives it may either choose a +2 experience bonus or +5 GBP income in the post-battle phase.

Each model may perform the search up to two times, but may not enjoy the benefits of multiple finds. Items or information recovered by a model may not be taken by opposing models unless the holding model is KO'ed.

If a model holding a relic or treasure is KO'ed, a friendly or enemy model may remove the item from his person at the cost of special action. The model that takes the item collects its benefit as long as it finishes the game with it in its possession.

Falling

A model within 1" of a battlement edge that does not have a wall risks falling if struck in close combat. Models successfully hit in close combat must make a TN3 Agility goal roll or plummet from the edge of the wall into the courtyard below. The normal rules for falling apply.

OBJECTIVE: Find as many relics among the ruins as possible while driving off the opposing warband.

END GAME: The game ends when one player has conceded, or all of an opposing Warband's opposition has been KO'ed. The game also ends if one warband finds four or more relics. At this point the opposition realizes that castle ruins have been picked clean and moves on.

SCENARIO REWARDS: +1 experience to winning warband members

SPECIAL EVENTS BOX	
1-2	Grudge Match
3-4	Ghostly Voices
5-6	Stygian Darkness

THE MANOR HOUSE

DESCRIPTION: This battle occurs amid the clutter and chaos of a rundown suburb in Prague. A minor cult of the Nameless Ones begins a dark ritual that they believe will grant them power. With the arrival of both warbands, the cultists flee, and the two groups of adversaries are left to battle over the mystical resources they have left behind.

SETUP: The battle transpires amid the detritus of a burned out manor house in one of Prague's rundown suburbs. The remains of the manor house should be placed in the center of the board, a roughly 1.5' x 2' building or series of connected buildings. Players should create a 5" diameter ritual circle in the center of the manor house. They can use small rocks, broken furniture, pieces of ceiling or wall, or anything else handy to delineate this circle.

Around the manor house's main section players should arrange other smaller buildings and terrain pieces to create corridors and blind spots. In all, the terrain should cover a 4' x 4' area.

Each player chooses a model to make a Mind + Sharp Senses goal roll. The model that scores more goals scouts the sight and chooses the best point of entry for his warband. Settle ties by re-rolling the contest until a winner emerges. The winning warband is then deployed within 8" of the board edge of its choice.

The losing warband must deploy on the opposite board edge, and in the same manner as the winning band.

SPECIAL RULES: Werewolf warbands will be uneasy amidst the clutter and pollution of Prague's soot-stained streets. All models in the band suffer -1" to their Move value.

The Ritual Circle! Like moths to flame, the warbands will be drawn to the ritual circle in the center of the manor house. Although the cultists who began the ritual have fled, the energies they have begun to unleash are still swirling about the room.

Any model that enters the circle may attempt to either halt the ritual or absorb some of the swirling power within it. Both count as special actions. Halting the ritual requires that model possess the Scholar trait, and requires a TN5 Mind + Scholar goal roll. Halting the ritual provides good fortune for the model, adding +3 Fate dice for the remainder of the battle.

Absorbing power from the ritual requires a TN4 Resolve goal and grants the model +4 Fate dice for the remainder of the battle. A model may only absorb power once, but may attempt to do so multiple times, spending a special action for each attempt.

OBJECTIVE: Drive the opposing warband from the warehouse and collect

Campaigns

what's left of the mystical booty, or in the case of band that opposes the Nameless Ones, interrupt the ritual and put it to a stop.

END GAME: The game ends when one player has conceded, or all of an opposing Warband's opposition has been KO'ed. Additionally, once the ritual is halted, either player may elect to quit the battle at the beginning of the next round.

SCENARIO REWARDS: +1 experience to winning warband members; +1 experience to the model that ends the ritual; +1 experience to any model that absorbs the ritual's power.

SPECIAL EVENTS BOX	
1-2	Artifact
3-4	Rare Book
5-6	Treacherous Agent

THE RESCUE

DESCRIPTION: This scenario details the attempted rescue of a captured warband mate or some other valuable individual. It could also depict a kidnapping attempt if the story of the campaign suits it. Players should run this scenario in the event of a Captured result on the post-battle tables presented below. It will allow them to raid an enemy warband's base and seize a comrade held hostage by their foes.

If this scenario is rolled where no member of either warband has been captured, another character becomes the center of the mission. This character could represent a valuable ally, family member, or savant holding special knowledge. Whatever the case, one warband holds the character hostage, while the other attempts to free him.

If the circumstances do not dictate it, players should randomly decide who the defender (the hostage holders in this scenario) and attacker (the liberators) will be. When a random

determination of this is called for, each player rolls a single die, and the high roller becomes the defender for the game.

SETUP: The battle takes place at a base or safe house controlled by the defending warband (the hostage holder). Players should utilize whatever terrain is available to set up a 12" square walled area where the hostage is being held. This area should sit roughly in the center of a 4' x 4' board.

The defending player sets up his warband in this area, with the exception of two models he nominates as sentries. These two models are placed on each of two of the board's edges.

The attacking player sets up his entire warband along one of the remaining two unoccupied board edges. He may deploy up to 4" in, and must set up the entire warband behind some sort of cover.

SPECIAL RULES: Sentries! The remainder of the defending warband cannot move or act until one of sentries sounds the alarm. The attacking warband counts as starting the game in hiding. The defending sentries may act normally, and once they spot one of the attacking warband's models, they may spend a special action to sound the alarm.

Spotting hiding models is a free action, but may only be attempted once per enemy model (up to the spotting model's Mind attribute).

Vampire models using Shape of the Bat may essentially hide in plain site, and receive +2D to their Agility goal rolls when resisting spot attempts.

Whether the sentries spot the attacking models or not, the alarm automatically sounds if the prisoner is released, or if any of the attacking player's models attack the defending warband.

Once the alarm has been sounded, the defending player may move his warband normally.

Campaigns

The Prisoner! The prisoner is bound and gagged, and may not be moved from his position in the setup area. The prisoner may be freed with a special action and may act normally on the round following its liberation.

If the prisoner is a member of the attacker's warband, he may be armed with an extra weapon from one of his liberators. If the objective is to rescue a character who is not part of the attacker's warband, players should use the stats for the Treacherous Agent listed in the special events section.

At no time prior to his release may the defenders harm the prisoner. This condition is removed the round after he has been freed.

OBJECTIVE: The defenders must prevent the hostage character from being rescued. The attacker must rescue the character and get him off of their starting board edge.

END GAME: The game ends when the hostage model exits from his warband's starting board edge.

SCENARIO REWARDS: +1 experience to winning warband members; +1 experience to the model who frees the hostage.

SPECIAL EVENTS BOX
1-2 Grudge Match
3-4 Rare Book
5-6 Stygian Darkness

THE CRYPT

DESCRIPTION: Rival bands clash amid the tight confines and pitch darkness of a subterranean crypt. The spoils awaiting the victor spur both groups into battle, but the price they pay may ultimately be too high.

SETUP: The battle transpires underground within a large, sprawling crypt containing the last remnants of one of Eastern Europe's great old households. The field of play for this battle is small, comprising a 2' x 2' area that should contain fallen columns, elevated stone crypts, and plenty of debris to act as cover.

Each player chooses a model to make a Mind + Sharp Senses goal roll. The model that scores more goals scouts the sight and chooses the best point of entry for his warband. Settle ties by re-rolling the contest until a winner emerges. The winning warband is then deployed 4" in the corner of the player's choice. The opposing warband is deployed up to 4" in the opposite corner.

SPECIAL RULES: Stygian Darkness! Normally a rolled special event, this effect automatically applies in this scenario.

Wealth of Ages! During the course of the battle any model may use a special action and make a TN4 Mind + Sharp Senses goal roll to search for booty. Each model may only attempt to search one time. A successful search means the model has a found a relic or other treasure worth extra money in the post-battle sequence. This is an ENC 1 item that model must finish the game with to earn the additional reward. If the model survives the battle with the item in its possession it may roll four extra dice during the post-battle phase when generating income.

Alternately, another model in the warband may take the item and add the dice to its roll. The item may also be stolen from the model if it is KO'ed during the course of the battle. A special action is required to lift the item from the unconscious model's possession.

OBJECTIVE: The opposing warbands must battle it out in close quarters, driving their enemies off to secure the wealth and artifacts that will help them continue their battles.

END GAME: The game ends when one player has conceded, or all of an opposing Warband's opposition has been KO'ed.

Campaigns

SCENARIO REWARDS: +1 experience to winning warband members; +1 experience to models who secure artifacts.

SPECIAL EVENTS BOX	
1-2	Ghostly Voices
3-4	Rare Book
5-6	Treacherous Agent

CONCEDING GAMES

There may come a time during a campaign game where a player deems it wiser to quit the field and live to fight another day. A player may choose to concede once he has suffered at least one KO or Coup de Grace. A player concedes at the end of a turn, after all models have acted, and before initiative is determined for the next turn.

At the point the player concedes the game ends. Any models embroiled in combats slip away, and any KO'ed models are carried off by their fellows. The conceding player loses the game and his opponent collects any remaining objective counters or other booty.

SPECIAL EVENTS INDEX

Listed below are the descriptions of the Special Events that could occur in the scenarios. Some special events will require players to roll randomly to determine if Warband members show up, benefit or suffer from some game effect, etc. Whenever a player is required to choose Warband members at random, each character in the Warband is assigned a number between 1 and 6, and a D6 is rolled to determine which model is chosen, affected, etc. If a Warband has fewer than six models, simply ignore higher die results and roll again.

ARTIFACT

Description: A valuable artifact from some past civilization is located on the battlefield. Place an appropriate counter or model for the Artifact in the center of the board. A model carrying it gains +1 Resolve. Models that suffer any Vitality loss while carrying the Artifact might drop it. A model injured while carrying the Artifact must make a TN2 Resolve + Iron Will goal roll or drop the Artifact where they stand. The Artifact is a 1 ENC item.

COMING OF THE DAWN

Description: The battle occurs close to the coming of the day. Starting with Round 3, the player who wins the initiative rolls a D6. On a result 6 the day breaks. Models susceptible to sunlight must seek shelter or suffer the consequences.

GHOSTLY VOICES

Description: The battlefield is haunted with restless spirits of its long-dead denizens, or perhaps the whispers of the Nameless Ones! The voices rise and fall in intensity from turn to turn. At the beginning of every Round, before initiative has been determined, one player rolls a single D6. On an odd result, no voices are heard that round, but on even result, the voices ring out loudly across the battlefield. When the voices are in effect, all models must make a TN2 Resolve + Iron Will goal roll or be partially stunned.

Models affected are at -2" move value and may not charge enemy models. They may still charge to cover extra ground. The effects of Ghostly Voices are cumulative with the effects of any failed Courage rolls (see Damage in PA in the Combat section). Whether they succeed in their goal rolls or not, once a model has heard the Ghostly voices for a turn, it becomes easier to resist their effects. In successive turns, models receive +1D to Resolve goal rolls to resist the effects of the voices. This benefit does not apply to Henchmen groups and normal Characters with the Cowardly special Trait.

GRUDGE MATCH

Description: Old rivalries fuel the conflict,

Campaigns

inspiring acts of savage brutality. All models in the battle receive +1D to Agility for close combat attacks.

RARE BOOK

Description: A rare tome is hidden in one of the buildings in this scenario. Models may enter any building and use a special action to search for it. Searching for the book requires a TN3 Mind + Scholar goal roll. A model that finds the book may pick it up as a special action; the book counts as an ENC 1 object. If a model finishes the game with the book in its possession it may choose to spend 1 Pulp point (from the next scenario's allotment) and study the book, making a Mind + Scholar goal roll and consulting the following table:

Goals	Results
0	Touch of Madness; -1 Resolve next scenario
1	Minor Insight; Gain 1 extra card on the first Initiative round next scenario, or add +1 die to Initiative
2	Deeper Mystery; Gain 1 extra card on the first two Initiative rounds next scenario, or add +1 die on the first two Initiative rounds
3	Higher enlightenment; +1 to Mind attribute next scenario
4+	Transfiguration: Model gains +1 Strength and +1 Agility, but also suffers -1 Mind and -1 Resolve (next scenario only).

A model may never consult a book more than two times. Once a book has been mined of its mysteries (i.e., studied twice) it may no longer be used by any member of the model's warband.

FALLEN TEMPLE

Description: Place a roughly 12" square ruin in the center of the table. This represents an ancient temple or church. It radiates an unsettling aura that must be overcome before a model may pas through it. Models may not enter the Fallen Temple unless they make a TN3 Resolve goal roll. Once a model makes this roll it need not make another for the remainder of the game, passing in and out of the temple area as it sees fit.

STYGIAN DARKNESS

Description: An inky, unnatural darkness blankets the battlefield and blocks much of the natural moonlight that might normally aid a normal human in perceiving his surroundings. Models subject to this event suffer -1" to their normal Move value and only receive +3" on a charge. Additionally, models receive +1D to Agility versus ranged attacks, and ranged attacks beyond 10" automatically miss their targets. Vampires, werewolves, and wolves are immune to this effect.

TREACHEROUS AGENT!

Description: One of the warbands has hired a model of dubious character that might betray it during the course of play. Players decide who has hired the Treacherous model by rolling off-the high die gets the potential traitor. The model is an expert in the acquisition of rare artifacts, and also knows how to handle himself in a fight. But he harbors a dark secret or hidden desire that could cause him to turn on his employers.

THE TREACHEROUS AGENT (50 GBP)

Str	Agl	Mnd	Res	Move	DR Pool	Fate	Vitality
2	3	4	4	5"	3	4	3

Special Traits
Crack Shot x 2
Combat Attack x 1
Scholar x 2

Equipment
Knife (DN4)
Light Pistol (DN4, 8")
Pack

Campaigns

A Treacherous Agent acts as a normal member of the player's warband until he receives either an Ace or a King for his Initiative draw, or the controlling player rolls no goals on an initiative check. Once this happens, the agent turns and acts as a member of the opposing player's warband! The opposing player should take his sheet and assume control of the model.

As his former employers do not yet know of his betrayal, they may not attack the Treacherous Agent until the after he has acted on the round in which he is dealt an Ace or a King. Players should use the stats on page 69 for the treacherous model.

POST-BATTLE RESULTS

Character models in Chaos in Carpathia can be knocked out or removed from the table during play. When playing a Campaign game, players should consult the appropriate Character Post-Battle Table to determine the extent of a model's injuries or condition.

KO'ed and Coup de Graced models must roll 1D6 on the table below to determine their fate. However, before rolling the player should roll the model's Resolve, with every two goals scored applying a +1 modifier to the die roll on the table. Coup de Graced models suffer a -2 penalty on their die rolls.

HUMAN POST-BATTLE TABLE

Roll	Result
0 or less	Dead!
1	Captured! Player should arrange Rescue mission scenario With his opponent
2	Badly Injured, miss next battle
3	Injured, -2" Move next battle
4-5	Minor Scrapes, no ill-effects
6	Vow of Vengeance +2 dice to attacks against warband that injured model during the next battle they face each other
7+	Inspired Recovery, +1 Experience

Campaigns

VAMPIRE POST-BATTLE TABLE

Roll	Result
0 or less	Destroyed!
1	Captured! Player should arrange rescue mission scenario with his opponent
2	New Vampiric Weakness (roll on table below this one)
3	Slow recovery -2" Move next battle
4-6	Minor Scrapes, no ill-effects
7	Vow of Vengeance +2 dice to attacks against warband that injured model during the next battle they face each other
8+	Inspired Recovery, +1 Experience

VAMPIRIC WEAKNESS TABLE

Roll	Result
1-2	Garlic (Foes possessing garlic gain +1 die on defense goal rolls versus the vampire.)
3-4	Running Water (The vampire may not cross running water with normal Move or Charge actions. Water less than 1" wide does not apply.)
5-6	Holy Symbols (Any model possessing a Holy Symbol gains +1 die on defense goal rolls versus the vampire.)

If a vampire rolls a result he already suffers from, his player should roll again until he gains one he does not. If he already suffers from all of the listed weaknesses, he instead loses 2 experience points.

WEREWOLF POST-BATTLE TABLE

Roll	Result
0 or less	Slain!
1	Captured! Player should arrange Rescue mission scenario with his opponent
2	Transitional form (Injuries cause werewolf to be trapped in a slightly weaker form for next battle: -1D to DR and Agility goal rolls)
3	Slow recovery -2" Move next battle, or -3" if it's a New Moon
4-5	Minor Scrapes, no ill-effects
6	Vow of Vengeance +2 dice to attacks against warband that injured model during the next battle they face each other
7+	Inspired Recovery, +1 Experience

GAMESMANSHIP AND VAMPIRIC WEAKNESSES

Through the course of a campaign vampires will naturally develop weaknesses, then buy them off, then pick up new ones. Opposing players running human warbands have the right to ask a vampire warband's player what weaknesses his models suffer from. This is the normal way of things in CIC; everything on an opponent's warband list is common knowledge.

However, a greater level of detail may be added if players decide they want it. If all players in a campaign agree to it, during any post-battle sequence a model possessing the Scholar trait may roll its Mind + Scholar dice versus TN4 to attempt to learn a specific vampire's weaknesses. If this method is chosen, a vampire's weaknesses are kept secret (while everything else on its sheet remains common knowledge).

Campaigns

THE VAGARIES OF CAPTURE AND DEATH: NOTES ON THE POST-BATTLE SEQUENCE

When a model is captured, the players involved must agree on a course of action using these rules as a guideline. Until he rescues or otherwise gets the model back, the player must play his games without the captured model. He does not have to pay any upkeep for the model, but the model obviously cannot work in the Resources phase of the post-battle. On the other hand, the model's captors must pay 1 GBP to feed and shelter him as if he was a member of the warband. This is offset by the fact that the model's equipment may be taken and sold for half its normal cost during the first post-battle after the model's capture.

The capturing player must allow the opposing warband one attempt to run the Rescue scenario at both players' earliest convenience. If the player fails to rescue his model, then the next course of action is up to the capturing player.

It is perfectly acceptable to arrange a ransom for the model. The capturing player may ask no more than the model's total cost plus his experience rating in GBP (less the cost of the model's equipment if the player chooses to keep or sell it instead of returning it). A player may also be kind to his opponent and allow the model to go for much less, or even allow him to escape for free.

In fact, players may skip the Rescue and go right to a ransom negotiation if both are amenable to such a course of action. If a rescue fails and a deal cannot be worked out, the capturing player never has to allow another rescue attempt and may hold the enemy model indefinitely. If a player randomly rolls a Rescue scenario and the defender turns out to be holding a model in custody, the player may elect to designate that model as his target for the rescue.

A warband may not hold more than two models in custody at time. If two models are held, the attacking player must decide which one to rescue, and the other is not present during the Rescue scenario.

Captured models may be sold into slavery (yes, even in the enlightened Victorian era the specter of slavery exists). A player receives half a model's starting cost, plus its experience in GBP for selling a model, and this occurs during the post-battle. In order to negotiate the sale, one of the warband's character models must forgo its resources roll to take the time to broker the sale.

How does one sell a monster? Well, the Vatican will pay handsomely for test subjects, and other less scrupulous individuals would love to experiment on supernatural creatures.

For human captives, it can very easily be imagined that their captors turn them into the authorities on some trumped up or legitimate charge, and collect a handsome reward for doing so.

Yet another alternative to rescue, negotiated ransom, and sale into slavery is execution. Even heroic bands may find it preferable to put a creature out of its misery rather than sell it into servitude or sentence it to death at the laboratory table.

HENCHMEN POST-BATTLE RESULTS

Henchmen groups that suffered casualties must determine if their fallen brethren recover, or are lost. A player rolls a D6 for each henchman in the group separately. On a 4+ the henchman recovers and is returned to the group. If the roll is less than four, he is lost. Henchmen groups that lose members can recruit new ones by purchasing their services. See Upkeep below for more details.

Campaigns

CAMPAIGN REWARDS

Character models that survive will eventually grow stronger, developing a formidable arsenal of attributes and special traits. Character models that survive battles and perform well earn experience points according to the following chart:

Survived Battle: 1 pt

KO Enemy Character Model: 1 pt

Defeat Enemy Henchmen: 1 pt
every 2 henchmen models taken out

Accomplish Scenario Objective:
usually 1 - 2 pts (see Scenario rewards for specifics)

Once a character model earns five (5) experience points it qualifies for an advance roll. Players roll 1D6 for their models on one of the tables indicated below. Vampires and Werewolves use the tables listed for them, while normal character models (including Blood Servants and most special characters) choose either the Combat Advance or Specialist Advance tables.

Most advances will indicate in parenthesis the number of times they may be taken. If a player rolls an advance he has already exhausted, he may roll again until he gets an advance his model can legally take.

COMBAT ADVANCE TABLE

Roll	Result
1	+1 Vitality (max +1)
2	+1 die Combat Attack (max +2)
3	+1 die Crack Shot (max +2)
4	+1 die KO Checks (max +2)
5	+1 Lightning Reflexes (max +2)
6	+1 die Combat Evade (max +2)

SPECIALIST ADVANCE TABLE

Roll	Result
1	+1 Sharp Senses (max +2)
2	+1 Scholar (max +3)
3	+1 die Fate (max Fate=3 x Resolve)
4	+1 Iron Will (max +2)
5	Gain Healer trait if model does not possess it, or +1 die Healer checks (max +2)
6	Choose desired result

VAMPIRE ADVANCE TABLE

Roll	Result
1	+1" Move Value (max 2)
2	+1 Use of Limited Use power (max 3)
3	+1 Vitality (max +1)
4	+1 die Combat Attack (max +2)
5	+1 Re-roll Resolve (max 2)
6	New Vampiric Ability (Choose from options in warband list; Limited Use powers start with one use)

WEREWOLF ADVANCE TABLE

Roll	Result
1	+1 Use Killing Strike (max +2 uses)
2	+1D Sharp Senses (max 3)
3	+1 Vitality (max +1)
4	+1 die Combat Attack (max +2)
5	+1 Re-roll Resolve (max 2)
6	Savage Frenzy (1 use, extra combat action when used, max 2) or New Werewolf Ability Choose from options in warband list; Limited Use powers start with one use)

HENCHMEN ADVANCEMENT?

Henchmen models do not earn experience in this way and always maintain the same stats.

TOTAL EXPERIENCE

Players should track the total experience their models have earned on their respective record sheets. Adding up a warband's total experience can give players a rough idea of how powerful their warbands are relative to other bands in the game. The number and quality of models a warband fields is also a valuable indicator of its potency.

POST-BATTLE RESOURCES

After each battle, every character model not taken out via Coup de Grace during the fight may work to gain resources for the warband. KO'ed models may work but roll 2 less dice than normal. The player decides which attribute to roll for each model, and each goal scored on the check earns the warband 2 GBP to spend on hiring new members, special

STEADIER INCOME

Some players may find the nature of the resource process too random for their tastes. For those who do, here is an alternative. Figure the number of dice the warband would roll for resources as normal, then halve that number and add an additional 5 GBP to the total. This is the warband's resource haul for that post-battle phase.

Other warband special income sources like the Resources trait are added to this total as normal. If players elect to use this method, they should do so together and stick to its use for the duration of the campaign.

Example: *Enrico's band has a total of 24 dice to roll for resources during this post-battle phase, but he and his fellow players have elected to use the Steadier Income option. He halves his 24 dice and gets 12, then adds 5 for a total of 17 GBP earned this post-battle.*

characters, or buying new equipment. Each warband maintains a treasury of funds that it can carry over from battle to battle.

Attribute rolls for warband members can be thought of as each member using his best talents to earn funds for the band. So a scholarly monster hunter might roll his Mind dice to gain resources, perhaps doing research for a local guild of academics, or a holy man might roll his Mind, sharing what he has learned of the Nameless Ones to gain greater support from church officials.

Whatever the source, a player gathers all of his resource dice together and rolls them as one great pool.

WARBAND UPKEEP

Every warband must pay to upkeep its holdings, feed its members, purchase new goods, replace fallen members, or hire special operatives. A warband pays its upkeep after each battle, following the resource gathering phase detailed above. In order to keep its holdings and members in good stead, a warband must pay 1 GBP for each character member in the band, and 2 GBP for each henchmen group. Players of human warbands (Monster and Treasure Hunters) must also pay a flat 2 GBP to maintain their base or headquarters. Monstrous warbands do not need to pay this fee, as their lairs arc often secreted in old ruins or wild places unknown to man.

SPENDING THE PROFITS

Anything a warband makes after covering its upkeep expenses can be used to pay retainers for existing special characters, purchase new weapons, equipment, members, special characters, or added henchmen for depleted groups. Players may also save some or all of their profits in their warband's reserve pool indicated on the warband roster sheet.

Players should use the costs listed in the equipment and weapons sections when buying new gear. New members can be added by using the costs in the warband section. New henchmen may be added to existing groups at the cost of 3 GBP each.

Campaigns

RARE ITEMS

Instead of working to earn money for the band, a model may spend its time between battles searching for rare items. In addition to paying the item's normal cost, the model must make a TN4 Mind + Scholar or Mind + Sharp Senses (whichever is higher) goal roll to successfully find the item.

The model only gets one chance between battles to attempt this roll, and failure indicates that the model was unable to find the desired item.

PAYING THE PIPER

If a warband does not generate enough income to cover its costs it suffers a shortfall. This manifests itself in decreased performance during the next battle. This decrease in performance could come from lack of ammunition, lack of provisions, or generally low morale due to the band's dire straits.

When a warband suffers a shortfall its player randomly selects two models to bear the brunt of it. The actual affects of the shortfall on the model depend upon the model's capabilities. Models with natural attacks like claws suffer privation and lose -1DN for their next battle. Models that rely on firearms or close combat weapons lose -1DN to their strongest weapon due to any number of factors (lack of ammunition, inability to pay for a good smithy, etc.).

Non-combat models, or models with True Faith or Scholar ratings of 2+ lose 2" from their Move value, as the band's lack of solid food stores or general unrest takes its toll on them.

Special characters are unaffected by this, and should not be included among the models randomly selected to suffer these effects.

PLAYING THE UNDERDOG

In campaign games warbands will sometimes find themselves facing a more powerful, numerous, and experienced foe. Some warbands run up on hard times, and need a bit of luck and incentive to face a tougher foes. This is what the Underdog Bonus has been designed for. Before facing off, players should consult the chart below to determine if one of them counts as an underdog for the battle.

The benefits conferred last for that battle only, but provide an extra edge during a game and extra rewards after for bands who find themselves in a weaker position.

Each player figures a Warband Experience Value (WEV) for his models after each battle. The higher the value, the better the warband. The WEV is simply the number of characters and henchmen groups (not individual group members!), plus the accumulated total experience divided by 5 (rounding up as usual).

Example: *A Monster Hunter warband consist of 1 Leader, 1 Slayer, 1 Holy Man and 2 Henchmen Groups. They have accumulated 14 Experience points. Their WEV is 5 + (14/5 = 2.8) = 8.*

The WEV may change after each game, because some members gain extra experience, are killed, or the player adds a new member.

UNDERDOG BONUS IN CAMPAIGN GAMES

When a warband fights against an enemy warband with a higher WEV, its warriors may get extra fate points for this one battle and may earn extra Experience points as shown on the table below.

The higher the opposing warband's WEV the more fate points and Experience points the underdog earns.

WEV Difference	Bonus Fate	Bonus XP
0-5	0	+0
6-10	1	+1
11-15	2	+2
16+	3	+3

Notes: Bonus fate points are per warband and must be allocated to individual characters before the battle. The bonus Experience points are per character.

Campaigns

AUTHOR'S THANKS

Chaos In Carpathia represents the work of many diverse hands. The book's roots lie in the SuperSystem series of games, but we would not have come to this point had it not been for the key contributions of the folks named in the front credits, and many others too numerous to list here in this volume. I would like to take time to thank Russ Dunaway from Old Glory, who has always believed in me and in my work. Russ has stuck with me through good and bad times, and I am proud to consider him my friend. I'd also like to thank my parents, Richard and Michele, who have little understanding of my obsession with toy soldiers, but support me nonetheless. All of the fine folks on the SuperFigs and Goalsystem Yahoo Groups also deserve thanks for their energy and ideas.

Aaron Tobul provided excellent editorial assistance, and Agis Neugebauer and Tom Weiss have been my most dedicated play-testers, and are two of the best darn painters whose work I have ever seen. I hope to actually game with them in Germany one day. J. Lee Howard will next carry the Goalsystem torch when he tackles the re-write of Chaos In Cairo, and he has provided much in the way of guidance for this work. Sweet Lou Reash lent his enthusiasm, his attic, and a city's worth of Miniature Building Authority terrain to our cause, and he deserves much credit for being with me from the beginning. Finally I want to thank my wife, JoAnn Rizzo, for her good grace and understanding of her husband's peculiar interest in painting miniatures and writing rules for them.

CHAOS
in
CARPATHIA

~8~

Appendix: Game Options and Play Aids

PLAYED AS WRITTEN CIC can be a fairly brutal affair, but the game engines finds its roots in the more cinematic and heroic style of our long-running superhero miniature combat game, SuperSystem. Players may want to incorporate one or all of the following options to change the tone of their games.

DICE FOR DAMAGE

Some players just like to roll dice, and players who prefer rolling for damage over the DN system presented here can convert the DN's of their models' attacks to dice by multiplying them by 1.5 and rounding the results to the nearest whole number.

Example: *A DN5 heavy pistol converted to the dice-based damage system would work as follows: 5 x 1.5=7.5, rounded up to 8. The player would roll 8 dice for the attack's damage.*

Special traits that add to DN's can still be used

Appendix: Game Options and Play Aids

by having them add dice to the normal total when they are spent.

Example: *A Werewolf with Killing Strike and an 8 dice close combat attack would roll 9 dice on turns when his player declares a use of the Killing Strike special trait.*

EXTRA ATTACKS

In this option models start every turn with two actions, and no distinction is made between special or combat actions. A model may use each of its actions to move up to its Move value. If a model uses both of its actions to move and finishes its move in contact with an enemy, it may count its move as a charge and attack with +2 dice. It still must move the last 3" in a straight line to get the +2 bonus. This double-action movement would then replace the normal charging rules.

A model already in base contact with foes when its turn begins may use each of its actions to attack. It may attack the same enemy twice, or split its two actions between two viable targets. In the same manner, a model that does not move may spend its two actions to fire a ranged attack twice. Again, it may split its attacks or concentrate one target.

In this system a model may still perform a number of free actions up to its Mind attribute.

EXTRA VITALITY

Most models begin play with only 3 Vitality. Players can ratchet up character survivability by adding +1 or +2 to all characters' starting Vitality totals. This will give character models a greater chance if they flub a damage resistance roll against a high DN attack.

EXTRA COMBAT GOALS

The default combat system rewards players with +1 to their Models' damage numbers if they beat their opponent's defense by 3+ goals. In these cases rolls exceeding the defense by 4+ are not really rewarded (except in the case of special weapons like wooden stakes).

Using this alternate rule, players in combat may take goals beyond 3+ and use them to accomplish specific effects. Warning, this does add a lot of extra detail (and time) to combats, but results in even more dynamic play options.

Drive-backs. Models in close combat may use extra attack goals beyond the first three to drive a foe back. Each extra goal spent in this fashion drives an opposing model back 1". Of course, if the model is KO'ed by the blow, it cannot move back! The attacking model follows, and gets to pick the direction, and at any point may stop 1" away from the model he is driving back.

This drive-back movement does not provoke free attacks, but can result in the model being driven off of a high precipice or ledge. The model in question may make the normal Agility goal roll to save itself from falling, but winds up hanging from the ledge with an enemy standing above it. Not good.

Example: *Aga makes a vicious knife attack on a vampire that beats the creature by 5 goals. The first 3 goals add +1 to the DN as normal, and Aga elects to use the remaining 2 goals to drive the vampire back 2".*

Called Shots. Models in close or ranged combat may elect to spend goals beyond 3+ to disable or hobble specific areas of a foe's body. The model must score at least 5 goals to do this (the normal 3+ to enhance the DN, and then 2 more for the called shot). The model may elect to hit one of the following areas, thus inflicting the noted penalties on the target:

Head (Stunned, TN4 Resolve + Iron Will goal roll or lose its Move next turn).

Torso (Bleeder, TN4 Resolve + Iron Will goal roll or suffer -1 Agility for the remainder of the battle. Models can suffer this effect a maximum of two times).

Arm (Weakened, TN4 Resolve + Iron Will goal roll or suffer -1 Strength for the remainder of the battle. Models can suffer this effect a maximum of two times).

Appendix: Game Options and Play Aids

Leg (Hobbled, TN4 Resolve + Iron Will goal roll or suffer -1" Move for the remainder of the battle. Models can suffer this effect a maximum of two times).

Knocked Down. Models in close or ranged combat may elect to spend goals beyond 3+ to knock a foe down. The model must score at least 5 goals to do this (the normal 3+ to enhance the DN, and then 2 more for the knock down).

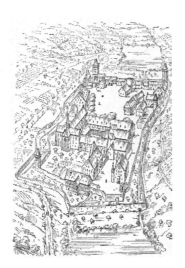

CIC WEAPON SUMMARY

Name	DN	ER	ENC	Special	Cost
Battleaxe	6	-	2	page 50	5
Club	3	-	1	-	3
Knife	4	-	1	-	4
Spear	4	5"	2	page 50	5
Sword	5	-	1	page 50	8
Th. Knife	3	3"	-	page 50	4
Wood Stake	3	-	1	page 50	2
Crossbow	5	12"	2	page 51	10
Holy Water	6	3"	-	Page 51	4
Pistol,Arch	4	8"	2	page 51	7
Pistol,Lt.	4	8"	1	-	8
Pistol,Hv.	5	10"	1	-	10
Rfile,Arch	5	12"	2	page 51	11
Rifle,Mod.	6	15"	2	-	16
Shotgun,S-O	4	5"	1	page 51	7
Shotgun	4	10"	2	page 51	10

DETAILED EXAMPLE OF PLAY

Here we provide a detailed example of several rounds of CIC action to give players a better handle on using some of the more complex special traits and interesting situations. This example details a small encounter between a group of Monster Hunters and a pair of vampires and their Cossack henchmen. The exact participants are:

Monster Hunters

Markus Riggs (Intrepid Leader, armed with knife light pistol, and stakes)
Father Tucker (Holy Man armed with knife, Holy Water, and light pistol)
Hans Gruver (Slayer armed with knife, stakes, sword, and shotgun)
Mentar the Mysterious (Mentalist armed with a knife)

Vampires

Count Adolphus (Romanian Vampire Lord armed with his claws)
Nadia the Dark (Lesser Vampire armed with a sword and claws)
Kanat the Turk (Blood Servant armed with a sword and light pistol)
The Count's Bodyguard (6 Cossack Henchmen armed with archaic rifles and knives)

The monster hunter player in this encounter is Lou, and the vampire player is Dan. The scenario is the Crypt from page 67 of the rules. The players roll and determine that the Ghostly Voices Special Event will be used. Lou chooses Hans the Slayer to make the Mind + Sharp Senses roll to scout the area and rolls 4 goals for him. Dan selects Count Adolphus and gets only 3 goals—Lou wins and chooses a corner of the board fronted by a large mausoleum to deploy his models behind. Dan then deploys his vampires in the opposite corner, a bit exposed amidst several fallen marble columns.

The special rules in this scenario are Stygian Darkness (ranged attacks beyond 10" fail automatically, and normal human models suffer -1" Move and reduced charges or 3"), Wealth of Ages (booty to be found on the use of a special action), and the special event

Appendix: Game Options and Play Aids

Ghostly Voices (roll before each new round, models make Resolve + Iron Will checks to avoid being stunned).

Before the players roll for initiative, Dan rolls a die for the Ghostly Voices and gets a 3—no models hear any voices this round.

Round 1

Each player then generates initiative totals using his leader model's Mind + Leader dice. Dan gets 2 goals for the Vampires and Lou generates 3 goals for the Hunters. Lou may choose the first activation, or defer to Dan. Lou seizes the initiative and activates Hans Gruver, the slayer. Hans charges to cover extra ground in the inky blackness of the crypt, adding 3" to his normal 5" Move score. He need not move the entire distance, but Lou runs him all out and places him 7" away behind a pile of rubble.

Dan takes the next activation and sends his Cossack Henchmen charging 7" toward a second mausoleum near the center of the board.

Lou next activates his Mentalist, Mentar, and moves him 4", then uses a special action for him to search for Wealth of Ages booty. He gets only once chance at this and it requires a TN4 Mind + Sharp Senses roll to succeed. Lou decides to increase his chances of success by spending one of Mentar's uses of Augury, adding an additional +2 dice to the try. He scores 6 goals and easily finds a rare jewel-encrusted goblet. Now he has to survive the battle with it to reap the benefits.

Dan then activates the Blood Servant Kanat and runs him 7" toward a distant pile of rubble, and also in the general direction of the mentalist and his valuable old goblet.

Perhaps sensing imminent danger, Mentar asks for some backup and Lou responds by sending his leader Markus Riggs charging 7" round the corner of the mausoleum in their starting area to guard the uneasy mentalist. Dan responds by sending his preternaturally swift vampire lord rushing 11" toward the other mausoleum near the center of the board.

Lou takes his last activation and sends his Holy Man Father Tucker rushing 7" after the slayer. He now has split his small force into two pairs of fighters.

Knowing the combat prowess of the slayer, Dan takes no chances and sends his lesser vampire Nadia rushing 11" after her master. Dan finishes the round with his two vampires and their Cossack henchmen rushing in the same direction toward the central mausoleum and an inevitable encounter with Riggs and Father Tucker. Meanwhile, Kanat the Turk hunts the Mentalist and the leader alone.

Round 2

Before initiative Lou rolls for Ghostly voices and gets a 2! A strange breeze whips up in the crypt and eerie voices raise the hackles on the necks of the fighters. All must make TN2 Resolve + Iron Will goal rolls. Only the unsteady Mentar fails the check, and he suffers -2" to his Move value in addition to the normal -1" for Stygian Darkness.

Dan wins the initiative this time 4 goals to 2, and elects to take the first activation with Kanat the Turk rushing another 7" round a pile of rubble. Again, moving toward the now stunned mentalist. Dan reasons that Kanat could reach him on a charge the following round.

Seeing this move, and reasoning that Mentar could hear the heavy footsteps of Kanat, or maybe even sense his evil intentions, Lou has the bedraggled Mentalist charge 5" back toward the mausoleum in his starting area.

Dan activates his Cossacks, rifles in hand, and runs them 7" into roughly the center of the board. They're dangerously exposed with no cover and an opposing model with a shotgun somewhere out there, but Dan is gambling that the Stygian Darkness will give them enough of an edge of defense to keep them alive.

Lou takes his activation, moving his leader Riggs 4" and raising his pistol for a shot at the

Appendix: Game Options and Play Aids

oncoming blood servant, Kanat. Checking the range, Lou finds Kanat within 10", but still beyond the effective range of the light pistol Riggs carries. He can shoot him, but the blood servant will receive +3 dice to defense (+1 for the darkness and +2 for being beyond the ER of the pistol). Lou gambles and adds a Fate die to Riggs' total attack dice pool, and rolls an impressive 6 goals on the throw. Even with his extra dice, Dan doesn't roll as well on defense, getting only 4 goals, and cursing his poor luck. Kanat is hit, but the shot isn't good enough to add to the gun's basic DN. He now rolls his DR versus the pistol's DN4, and gets 3 goals, suffering 1 Vitality loss.

With that Dan unleashes his big guns! He sends Nadia charging 11" into the slayer Hans Gruver. Having started 4" in and run 11" on her previous turn, her subsequent charge this turn gives her more than enough movement to reach the hunter on the crypt's tightly confined 2' x 2' battle area. Wielding her sword instead of her claws, she channels one use of her Vampiric Might and slashes at Hans, scoring 7 goals on a vicious attack. Hans defends with only 4 goals and suffers a nasty DN8 hit (Sword is DN5, +1 for Nadia's Strength, +1 for succeeding by 3+ goals, and +1 for Vampiric Might). Knowing how tough this DR roll will be, Lou adds all 3 of Hans' Fate dice to his roll, for a total 8D[1] (the re-roll comes from Hans' Tough special trait). He manages an amazing 6 goals, losing two of his three Vitality points but avoiding the dreaded KO check.

Deciding that Hans must strike back before Dan also charges Count Adolphus into the fray, Lou activates the slayer next. He decides using a stake at this point is too risky, and for a free action pulls his trusty knife instead. He attacks and scores a solid 5 goals, but Nadia fails to match him, scoring only 3 goals on defense. She must now roll her DR versus DN5 (Knife is 4 +1 for Hans' Strength of 4). Dan curses as he flubs the roll, scoring only 2 goals again and losing all 3 of Nadia's Vitality in the bargain! Now she must make a TN3 KO check to remain standing. Here Dan spends all 3 of her Fate dice to add to the roll, deciding

that leaving any Fate dice potentially unused is a bad idea. He rolls and scores 5 goals—Nadia remains standing, albeit shakily. Any further damage will drop her instantly. Now Dan unleashes Count Adolphus, the most dangerous model on the table! He charges Hans (no surprise there) and enjoys +3 dice to the attack (+2 for charging and a +1 friends bonus for Nadia also being in close combat). Dan also announces that he will spend one of the Count's two uses of Vampiric Might. He attacks and scores a whopping 7 goals. Hans defends and manages 5 goals, denying the Count a further +1 to his DN. Still, the Count's claws are deadly and Hans must roll DR versus DN7 (DN6 claws +1 for Vampiric Might). Hans only gets 3 goals, and the 4 points that go through easily wipe out his remaining 1 Vitality point. He must now make a TN3 KO check. He rolls his three Resolve dice and initially scores only 2 goals, but because he is Tough, he gets a re-roll on KO checks, and gets another goal on the re-roll. Hans is still up, but only just.

Now it is time for Father Tucker to shine, Lou thinks. For a free action he pulls his holy symbol and stalks forward 4" toward mighty melee between Hans and the two vampires. Knowing that Nadia is both hurt and weaker-willed than the Count, he uses his True Faith against her, trying to force her from the combat. Lou checks the range and sees that Nadia is exactly 3" away, within the ER of the attack. He rolls the holy man's Resolve + Iron Will and Dan rolls Nadia's Resolve. Lou wins 4 goals to 1, and Nadia must flee 6" from the sight of the cross and the power of Father Tucker's faith! Hans does not get a free attack because he is outnumbered in close combat.

Sensing the desperation of the moment, Lou remembers than he can spend 2 Fate dice to perform an additional special action (see page 6), and does, brandishing his cross again, but this time at Count Adolphus. Adolphus is 5" away, so he receives +2D to his Resolve for defense. Both players agree that because a vampire's senses render it immune to darkness, Adolphus will not receive a further +1 for this condition. The players roll off and Father

Appendix: Game Options and Play Aids

Tucker wins again, 3 goals to 2. The Count retreats only 2", but Hans still cannot attack, as he suffered damage from the Count's attack this round and is still back on his heels (see pages 14-15, Breaking From Close Combat).

Round 3

Dan rolls a 1 for Ghostly Voices and the maddened cries fade from the battlefield. The players then roll for initiative and both score 3 goals—a tie! They compare Mind scores and the Count's ancient reservoir of wisdom (and Mind of 4) breaks the tie, Dan has first choice.

Dan knows he must finish the slayer now, so he activates Count Adolphus, announces he

is spending his last use of Vampiric Might, and readies to charge the teetering Hans. But sensing the danger of his comrade, the now recovered Mentar the Mysterious spends his last use of Augury and acts before the Count (see Augury page 39). Dan frowns but nods for Lou to continue, and he charges Mentar 7" around the mausoleum, getting to within 10" of Hans the slayer. As a free action he gives Hans 5 of his 7 Fate dice, sending him positive emanations using his Gypsy's Luck special trait (see page 40). Smiling, Lou nods for Dan to continue.

A very angry Count Adolphus now moves back into combat with Hans. He cannot benefit from a charge because he must move

Appendix: Game Options and Play Aids

at least 3" in a straight line toward his foe, and he is only 2" away. But he also elects to add 2 Fate dice to his attack. Meanwhile, Lou adds 3 of Hans' newly gifted Fate dice to his defense, and manages to tie the vampire lord 4 goals to 4. Defenders always win ties, so he beats the Count's attack back. However, seeing that the Count has 2 Fate remaining, Dan decides to spend them to give the count a second attack. This time he hits! Lou adds Hans' two remaining Fate dice to his DR roll, but flubs it and goes down! Dan puts a check mark on the Count's profile to remind himself that Count gets credit for KO'ing and enemy model.

Sensing that the tide is shifting, Lou now activates his leader, moves 4" forward, and takes a shot at the Cossacks in a desperate attempt to pin them and reduce their combat effectiveness. He doesn't want to lose Father Tucker, and he knows the Cossacks now have him in their sights. He fires, and even with darkness and the range penalty, manages to slay one Cossack with two points of Vitality loss left over. The Cossacks must now make a TN3 (1 + 2 for extra Vitality loss) Resolve check or be pinned. They fail and anyone they fire at will now receive +1D to attack and defense against them. They also suffer -2" Move.

Dan next activates the Cossacks and they fire at Father Tucker. He moves them their max of 1" (Slow weapons and Pinned) to try to get them into range, but when he checks this leaves them at 11" and the shot automatically misses.

Lou then activates Father Tucker and he moves forward 4" to use his True Faith on Nadia. He wins and drives her back an amazing 10", and out of charge range.

Dan charges Nadia towards Markus Riggs, Lou's leader, reasoning that if the combat goes another round she might have a chance to aid Kanat against him. She's also had enough of Tucker's True Faith.

Without any other activations this round, Lou defers again and Dan activates his blood

servant, who charges Riggs, hits, and scores 2 Viatlity points from the hit.

That seals it for Lou. He doesn't want to risk any further losses, and concedes the game. Mentar keeps his goblet, and both players agree that each member of the vampire band can make one search roll for the Wealth of Ages. They then proceed to the post-battle.

BLUE MOON MANUFACTURING MINIATURE STOCK CODES:

BMM100 Box 1 "I Had Such a Howling Good Time" - A Werewolf Scenario (12 figures for $26.00)

BMM101 Box 2 "You're Such a Pain In The Neck" - A Vampire Scenario (12 figures for $26.00)

BMM102 Box 3 "I Just Don't Feel Put Together Right" - A Frankenstein Scenario (12 figures for $26.00)

BMM103 Box 4 "I Just Don't Feel My Age" - A Mummy Scenario (12 figures for $26.00)

BMM104 Box 5 "The Streets of London" - A Jack The Ripper Scenario (12 figures for $26.00)

BMM105 Box 6 "I'm Loosing My Head Over You":- A Legend Of Sleepy Hollow Scenario (12 figures for $26.00)

BMM106 European Timber Wolves (12 figures for $26.00)

BMM107 Romanian Villagers (20 figures for $40.00)

BMM108 American Colonial Villagers (20 figures for $40.00)

BMM109 London Victorian Civilians (20 figures for $40.00)

ORDERING INFORMATION

Blue Moon Manufacturing
Box 20, Rt. 981
Calumet, PA 15621
1-724-423-3580
http://www.bluemoonmanufacturing.com
teresa@bluemoonmanufacturing.com

Chaos in Carpathia Warband Roster

Warband Type _____

Warband Name _____

Treasury _____

Location of Lair _____

WEV _____
(# members + total xp/5)

Name _____

Type _____

MV	DR	Str	Agl	Mnd	Res	Fate

Vitality ○ ○ ○ ○ ○ ○

Special Traits _____

□□□□□ _____ _____
□□□□□ _____ _____
□□□□□ _____ _____
□□□□□ _____ _____

Equipment

Experience □□□□■ □□□□■ □□□□■ □□□□■ □□□□■ □□□□■
□□□□■ □□□□■ □□□□■ □□□□■ □□□□■ □□□□■

Total Cost =

Name _____

Type _____

MV	DR	Str	Agl	Mnd	Res	Fate

Vitality ○ ○ ○ ○ ○ ○

Special Traits _____

□□□□□ _____ _____
□□□□□ _____ _____
□□□□□ _____ _____
□□□□□ _____ _____

Equipment

Experience □□□□■ □□□□■ □□□□■ □□□□■ □□□□■ □□□□■
□□□□■ □□□□■ □□□□■ □□□□■ □□□□■ □□□□■

Total Cost =

Name _____

Type _____

MV	DR	Str	Agl	Mnd	Res	Fate

Vitality ○ ○ ○ ○ ○ ○

Special Traits _____

□□□□□ _____ _____
□□□□□ _____ _____
□□□□□ _____ _____
□□□□□ _____ _____

Equipment

Experience □□□□■ □□□□■ □□□□■ □□□□■ □□□□■ □□□□■
□□□□■ □□□□■ □□□□■ □□□□■ □□□□■ □□□□■

Total Cost =

Name _____

Type _____

MV	DR	Str	Agl	Mnd	Res	Fate

Vitality ○ ○ ○ ○ ○ ○

Special Traits _____

□□□□□ _____ _____
□□□□□ _____ _____
□□□□□ _____ _____
□□□□□ _____ _____

Equipment

Experience □□□□■ □□□□■ □□□□■ □□□□■ □□□□■ □□□□■
□□□□■ □□□□■ □□□□■ □□□□■ □□□□■ □□□□■

Total Cost =